# Knowing My Audio System

## A window to live sound

## Author:  José (Naldy) Resto



First Impression: 2017

ISBN: 978-0-9975351-2-9

José E. Resto
restomusic@gmail.com

www.restomusicpro.com

# Dedication

This manual, *Knowing my audio system: A window to live sound*, has been a product of experience, study, hours of practice and multiple activities where we have performed live sound. But this is possible thanks to God, to whom I dedicate this work first, who has given grace and knowledge, and to whom I owe everything.

To my wife, Miriam Cuadrado, who has been an unconditional companion throughout this journey, for her sleepless nights, her effort and for being a help.

To all those friends who are part of my growth and who have shared their knowledge.

To the church "Iglesia del Peñón", where I grew up, I developed and I learned to love God above all things; for their testimony, and those who have witnessed my growth.

To my family, Resto-Cuadrado, who have always been involved in all our steps, and their advice and experiences have accompanied me throughout this trajectory.

Thanks to my sister Merari, my nephew Jeremy Camey and our friend Mary Ann Ramos, for the translation of this manual.

To Ray and Marie Vázquez, for being the mentors of this project and who have been motivation and guides to make this work a reality.

*José (Naldy) Resto*

# Index

# Introduction

The preparation and development of an activity or program leads us to the need to use a sound system with which we will cover more people. Whether in concerts, churches, conferences, weddings, social activities, assemblies, birthdays, etc., it would be difficult to develop the activity without a sound amplification.

The sound system will be responsible for amplifying and distributing the sound generated by some source. The sources can be for example: a speaker, a singer, an instrument, an object, etc. The intensity or volume of the sound generated by the source is very low level, which will only reach those people who are close to the source. By means of an adequate amplification of the sound generated by the source, we can reach a greater number of listeners. That the amplification is adequate or not, could be due to many factors.

One of them is the venue or the structure, which is built primarily to bring together many people, but it is not prepared correctly to use a sound system, like installing acoustic on the ceiling, walls with sound absorption panels and floors with carpet.

The structure has power supply to cover the basic operation of the venue, such as lighting and appliances, but does not have the appropriate electrical connections to install a sound system either permanently or mobile.

Another factor that directly affects the sound is the noise generated by the equipment installed in the structure, for example, compressors and fans of the air conditioning system, which in many cases generate a lot of noise affecting the sound equipment performance.

Other times the activity is done outdoors, where we experience environmental noise, generated by vehicles, excessive external music, industrial machinery and all that generated noise that directly interferes with our audio system.

This manual is a practical guide to know, install and operate an audio system. In addition, you can make the necessary modifications in a system already installed. This manual is presented in a complete but simple way, including my experience of many these years as a musician, sound technician and sound systems installer in different institutions.

We will take a trip that will guide us step by step and where we will focus on the fundamental and technical elements in an easy way to understand and quick to perform. It is necessary that you finish all the steps so that you have the complete map, from fundamentals of the electrical system to audio signal processing.

It is not just an encounter, but a journey. So, get comfortable and let's begin.

# Chapter 1: The Sound

The relation that we have directly with any sound is due to the ability to listen. We all possess one of the most sophisticated sound processors: our ears. If we did not have ears, the sound would be irrelevant, since in the absence of hearing, we would not have a measure or parameter to identify and classify the sounds.

The vibration of an elastic medium produces **the sound** by definition. The elastic medium can be solid, liquid or gaseous. Examples of an elastic medium are the vocal cords, the strings of a guitar, the leather of a drum, shock of a drop of water or blowing a flute. In all these examples, a vibration takes place. The sound is **produced** by vibration, which in turn moves air molecules where the sound travels in the form of waves (**transmission**) and reaches the ear, which is the recipient (**reception**) (Figure 1.1).

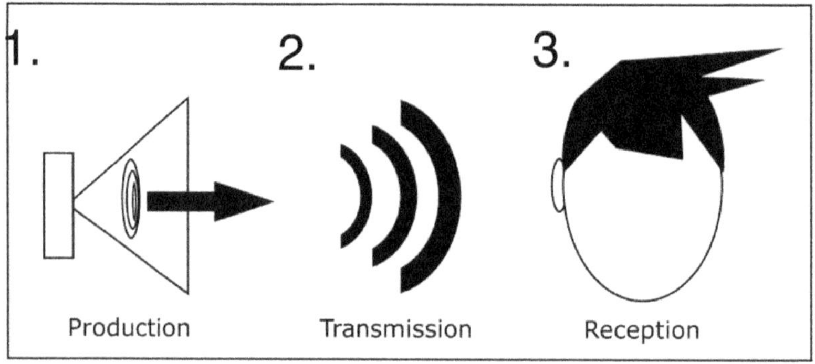


Figure 1.1
¿How sound is produced?

The way in which the sound is produced and transmitted will depend largely on the perception (listening skills) and knowledge of the person responsible for managing the audio equipment (soundman). This is because the **human factor**, along with the adequate equipment, will result in an exceptional amplification between the **source**, or the one who generates it and the **audience,** who receives it.

<u>The nature of sound:  Sound Wave</u>

As it was mentioned earlier, the ***transmission of the sound*** consists in the propagation of a variation in the air pressure.  Let us look at this example, which explains the movement of a speaker cone while reproducing a sound.

When there is no movement of the cone, there is no variation in the pressure of the air, and there is no presence of sound (Figure 1.2).

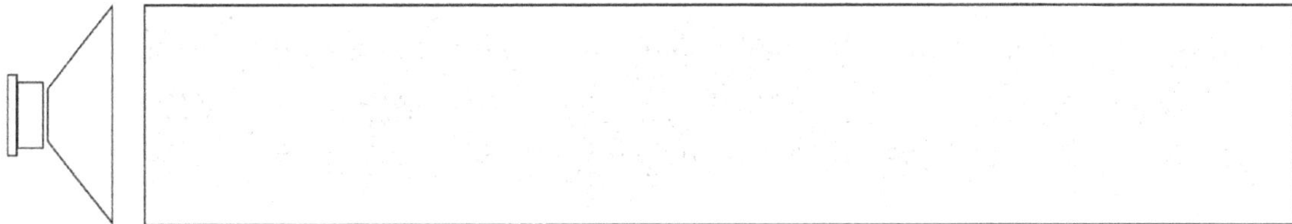

Figure 1.2

When the cone is moved outward, the air that is immediately in front of the cone is compressed beyond its normal pressure.  The compressed particles are moved forward by exerting a pressure in the air that is in front of it.  This is known as a ***wave of compression*** (Figure 1.3).

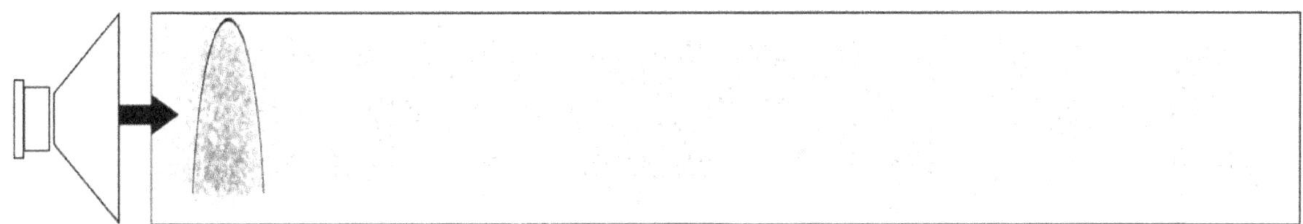

Figure 1.3

When the cone moves to the interior, it partially creates an effect of a "***vacuum***", or expansion.  At this time, the particles in the air move rapidly towards the interior when the expansion is generated.  This is known as a ***wave of expansion*** (Figure 1.4).

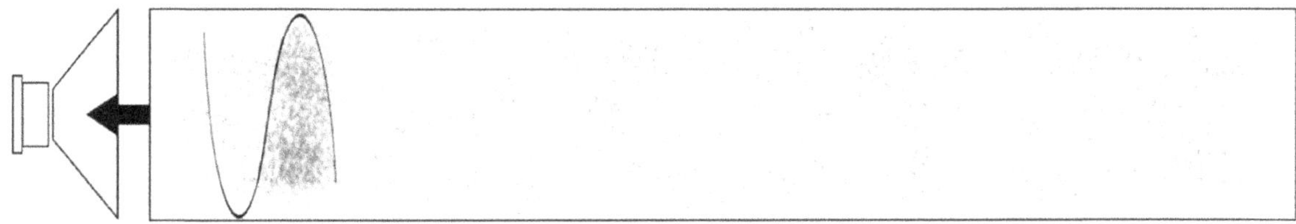

Figure 1.4

<u>Cycle</u>

Whenever the cone has completed a forward movement and a backward motion, returning to its point of origin, a **cycle** has been completed (Figure 1.5).

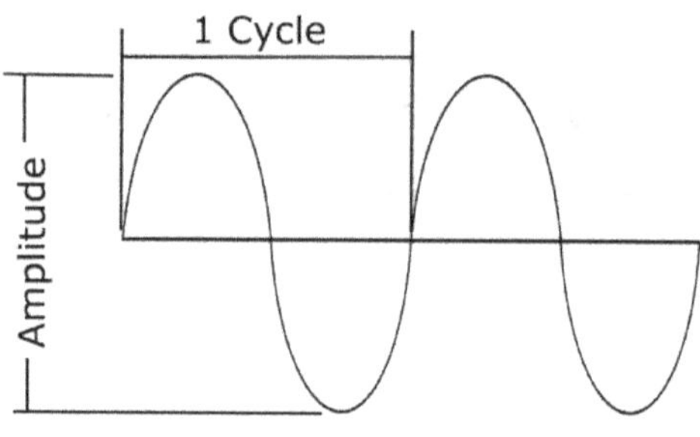



*Figure 1.5*

While the cone continues moving in the same way, it will generate a series of rapid compressions and expansions, creating a variation in the air pressure as a domino effect.  This will be perceived by our ears, which will detect it and interpret it as a particular sound (Figure 1.6).

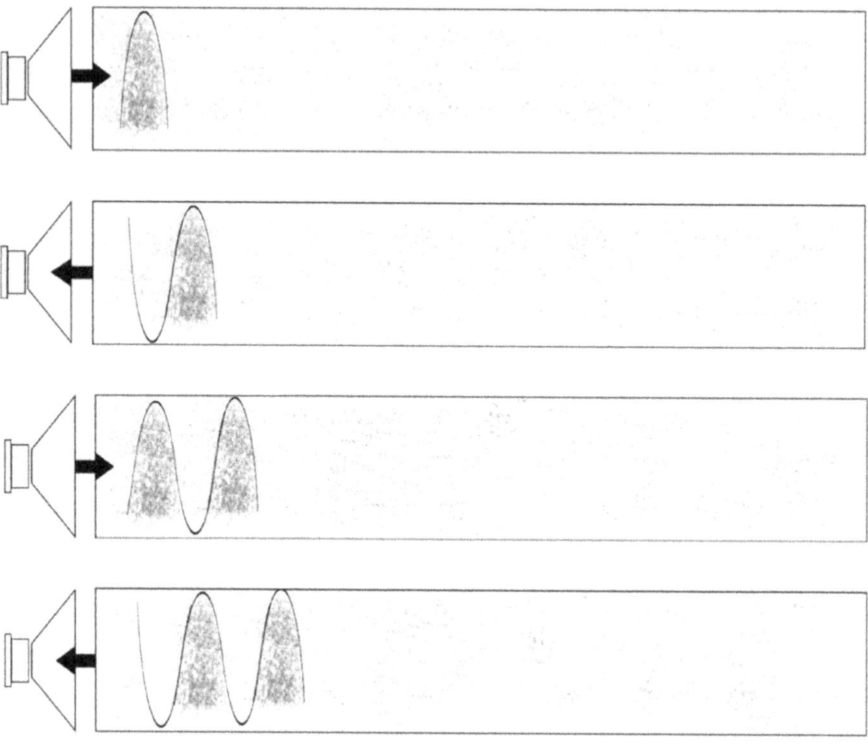

*Figure 1.6*

This variation generates a movement of air in the form of a wave.  To describe how the wave is formed, let us look at this example:

*Imagine a fish bowl with water, but no movement, in total rest.  Then we drop a stone.  The result of the impact of the stone with the water will result in the formation of waves, which will propagate from the point of origin to the walls of the bowl.*

The spread of a sound works in the same manner.  When the variation of the air pressure happens, there is a movement of the molecules in the form of waves and this is known as a ***sound wave.***

## Characteristics of the air

The air has other relevant features for sound propagation:

- the ***linear*** spread, where different sound waves can propagate at the same time for the same space, without affecting each another.
- the ***non-dispersive medium***, the sound waves propagate at the same speed regardless of its amplitude or frequency.
- the ***homogeneous medium***, the sound propagates spherically, in all directions, generating a sound field.

# Chapter 2:  Frequency

We have already seen that the variation in air pressure produces a sound wave. Each sound has a number of pulsations (every pulsation completes a cycle), and depending on the quantity of pulsations, the sounds are classified as lows, mid or highs.

The definition of **frequency** is the number of pulsations (cycles) that a sound wave has per unit time.  That is, the number of times a wave oscillates in a second, and the unit used for frequency will be the unit, hertz (Hz).

When the repetition (pulse) of a sound wave occurs 20 times in a second, this will be expressed as 20 hertz, and abbreviated as 20Hz.  A 20Hz frequency will represent a sound in the whole spectrum of hearing (Figure 2.1).

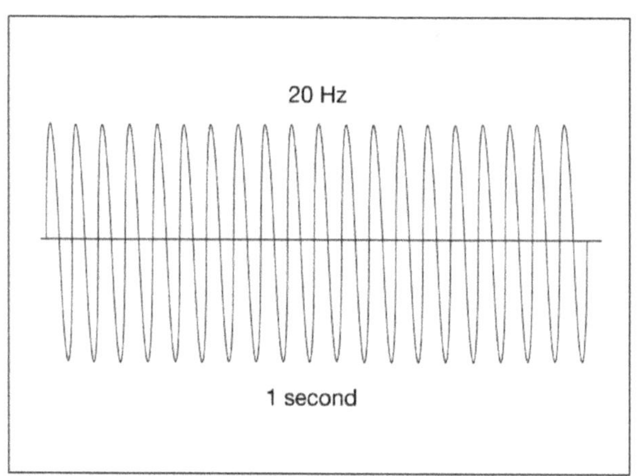


*Figure 2.1*
*Example of 20 cycles per second*

The unit used for frequency will be the hertz, and its symbol is (Hz), in honor of the German physicist Heinrich Hertz who discovered radio waves.

## The audible spectrum of human being

The human being does not hear all existing sounds.  The human ear does not perceive sounds very low and sounds very high.  The deeper sound that the human being can perceive is 20Hz, and the sharper sound is of 20,000Hz (Figure 2.2).

20Hz ——— 20,000Hz

Low High

*Figure 2.2*

To shorten 20,000Hz we use the abbreviation of thousand *kilo* (k), and express it as 20kHz. All frequencies above 1,000Hz use the abbreviation for *kilo.*

Examples:

- 1,000Hz = 1kHz
- 2,500Hz = 2.5kHz
- 10,000Hz = 10kHz

## Audible frequency table of human beings in Hz

These frequencies are divided as follows: 20Hz is the lowest or deepest frequency and 20kHz is the highest or sharpest frequency (Figure 2.3).

High frequencies

| | | | | | | | | |
|---|---|---|---|---|---|---|---|---|
| 3.15k | 4k | 5k | 6.3k | 8k | 10k | 12.5k | 16k | 20k |

Medium frequencies

| | | | | | | | | | | |
|---|---|---|---|---|---|---|---|---|---|---|
| 250 | 315 | 400 | 500 | 630 | 800 | 1k | 1.25k | 1.6k | 2k | 2.5k |

Low frequencies

| | | | | | | | | | | |
|---|---|---|---|---|---|---|---|---|---|---|
| 20 | 25 | 32 | 40 | 50 | 63 | 80 | 100 | 125 | 160 | 200 |

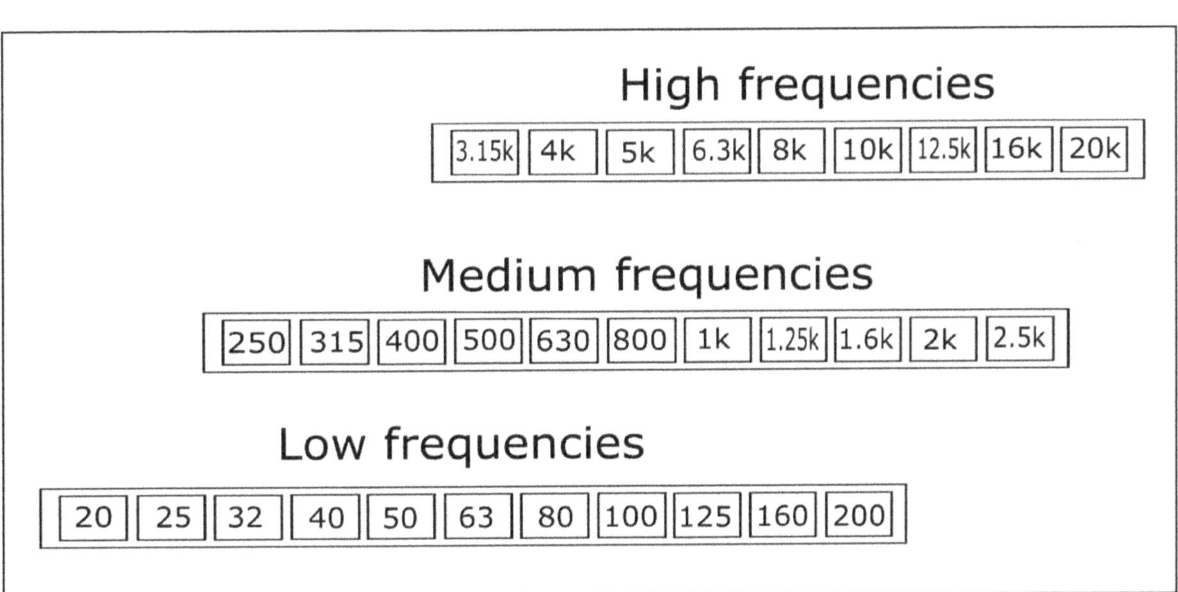

*Figure 2.3*
*High, mid and low frequencies*

# Chapter 3:  Hearing:

## Essential Basis of the Sound Technician

We hear, because our ears were designed to have auditory contact with what is around us, whether the sound is produced by nature, the human voice, and a musical instrument or reproduced by electronic audio equipment.  As we see and we can identify and separate the colors, the same happens when a sound reaches us; we can **identify it, classify it and separate it**:

- *identifying*   *:* where is comes from (What direction?)
- *classifying*   *:* what is the source (Who generates it?)
- *separate*    *:* it is low, medium or high (Which is the frequency range?)

It is wonderful what we can achieve listening, but we often limit what we hear, not paying attention to what is coming to our ears.  We do not deepen and train our ears to identify and separate every source that generates a particular sound.

The ear, in addition to serve as a mean of communication, also immerses us in the beauty of the appreciation of melodies produced around us, thus separating what is noise and what is harmonious.

- *melody*: it is the part of the composition, which develops a musical idea executed by the voice or an instrument.

- *noise*: sound or unwanted signal that contaminates the sound generated by our audio system; this could be a machinery noise, vehicles in the street, people talking, etc.

We can hear a particular sound, like a whistle in a game of basketball, but we hear much more than individual sounds, we listen to a wide range of frequencies, volumes and qualities or timbres.  Therefore, the main instrument that every sound engineer uses to "mix" is the ear.

*Mixing*, it is the process in which different voices and instruments are combined in a soundboard.  First, the audio signal is received on the mixer to go through a process of management in which it is amplified, equalized, filters are added, an individual volume is assigned, and when all the signals are combined, the mixing is completed.  There is no equipment to replace hearing appreciation.

**The way we hear sounds in the audio system will be primarily influenced by how we have trained our ears.**

Remember that the audio system is the processing channel, where we capture, amplify and distribute the sound.  What comes out of the speakers will be primarily affected by the way we listen.

Some instruments or voices are more predominant in a frequency range than others, although they are not limited.  To provide an example that we can use as a base to start, we will divide it as follows:

- In low frequencies you will find: bass, trombone, cello, kik drum
- In the mid and high frequencies: voice, guitar, flute, alto saxophone, percussion
- In high frequencies: bells, triangles, "güira", cymbals, percussion instruments

# Chapter 4:  Train Your Ear

One of the ways in which we can begin to train our ears is listening to recordings of musicians and solo singers.  **Soloist** is the person who plays a solo in a musical piece, either vocal or instrumental (rae.es).  When we hear the recording of a soloist, an instrument or voice stands out above the musical base.

## The process of identifying

The importance of this is that we begin to hear the instruments and voices individually, which will help us:

1. Identify the instruments by its timbre
   - **timbre**, is the quality of sound by which we can distinguish one instrument from another, even if they are playing the same note.
     Example: we can differentiate the bass from a saxophone even if they are playing the note 'A' (440Hz) at the same time.
2. Listen to the instruments or voices by their range
   - low range
   - middle range
   - high range
3. Hear how the instruments generate their own sound from an acoustic appreciation.
     Example:  the sound generated by the body of the acoustic guitar

*I want to emphasize that the process of mixing can have many variations, just like the art of painting has.*

When painting, we can use the same colors as the basis, but when the colors are mixed, it will open a window of color shades alternatives that provides the artist with a world of possibilities.

That is how the sound mix works.  It is an art.  It is like watching a canvas in which we begin to place the instruments in different positions, classification, and mixing them at different volume levels.  This will depend on the management, knowledge and training that the sound engineer has.


## Basic musical mix

When we are working in audio mixing, not all voices, instruments or sounds are at the same volume.  Some will be heard stronger, with more presence than the others.  One will carry the main melody and the others will form the base.

Consider this example in Figure 4.1:

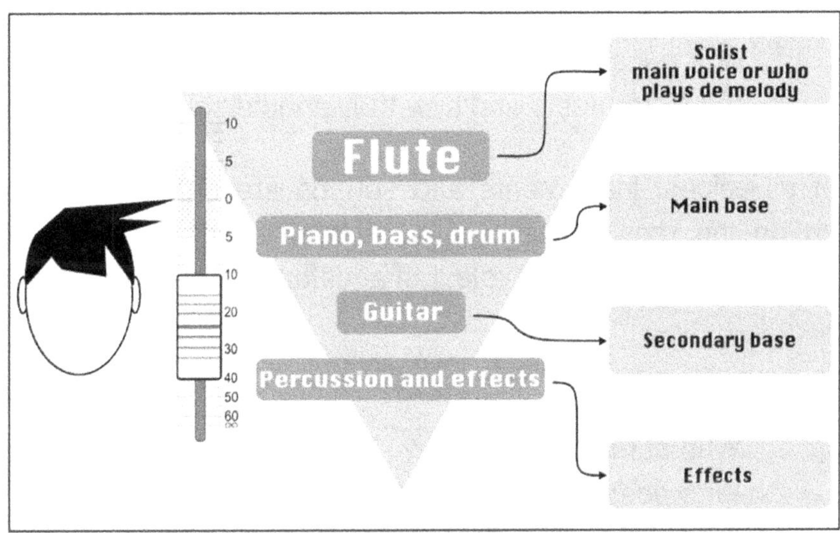


Figure 4.1

In this piece of music:
1.  the flute carries the melody or main voice
2.  the harmony and rhythms is carried by the drums, bass and piano
3.  the guitar, which is in secondary base, can move between small melodic phrases, rhythmic accompaniment or reinforcing the harmony base
4.  the percussion and the effects (such as "pads" of violins on an electric synthesizer), complement what you hear in the background of the musical piece.

This is just one example of the possibilities that may exist.  The training of your ear is a task that you have to start developing.

<u>How to train your ear</u>

These recommendations will help you to raise the level in the process of listening:

1. Do not listen to the music too loud, eventually you will begin to lose hearing.
2. Stay away from noises such as drills, industrial machineries and everything that can damage your hearing.  Use protection.
3. Listen to various musical genres so you can have a better assessment and interpretation when making a mix.  A jazz band is not mixed like a rock band.
4. In a song, learn how to listen to the instruments individually, such as the guitar, drums, percussion, bass, etc.
5. Listen to recordings of musicians by instruments.  Example: recording of a guitarist or drummer, so that you can start defining and knowing the instruments and how they should sound.

Not all voices, instruments and sounds are set at the same volume level. Depending on the musical genre (i.e., if tropical genre, rock, ballad, etc.), each instrument will play an important role, but at different levels, according to what you are projecting.

Listen carefully:

1. Who carries the melody?
2. Who does the base?
3. Who makes the effects?

# Chapter 5: Where It All Begins

One of the most important issues when we talk about an audio system is the beginning.  What beginning? you might ask.  It does not start when we decide to buy speakers, a mixer, microphones, cables, etc.  It is not because we like listening to music, or because we have an audio player, or because we bought it and that is all.

No, it really starts with a need generated in the moment in which we want to reach more people to listen to something that we are going to impart, whether it is information, a message, music, advertisement, education, amplifying a band, the entertainment for a wedding, or any sound you want to generate to a larger scale.

Amplification of sound is to take a sound from a smaller scale to a larger scale; it starts with the need to reach more people in a given area.  For this reason, we find a larger location or space to carry out our mission, but the number of people that we are going to impact is not the only factor to consider.

The venue, may have 100 or 500 people, but is the place properly prepared for what we want to share?  I am not saying that the place should have things like a water fountain, freezer or bathrooms.  If you want more people to hear what you have to share, it will require that you install or hire a sound technician with his audio system. You also have to investigate if the acoustics of the place helps the system and if the electrical connections are sufficient for this.

These two elements are very important when choosing a place to celebrate an activity.  It is where we usually fail and make mistakes.  The place can be cute, have the best decorations, have crystallized floors, European lamps, but you do not do more than put a speaker and this becomes a whole disaster.  The complaints and comments start, they tell to the sound technician "it does not sound good."  What can we do? Well, first, you have to know and then you can do.  If you are developing a program in place, you have to take into consideration all the elements; and the first is the venue, location of participants and location of recipients.

## The venue

These are the different structures or venues that you will find when installing an audio system (Figure 5.1).

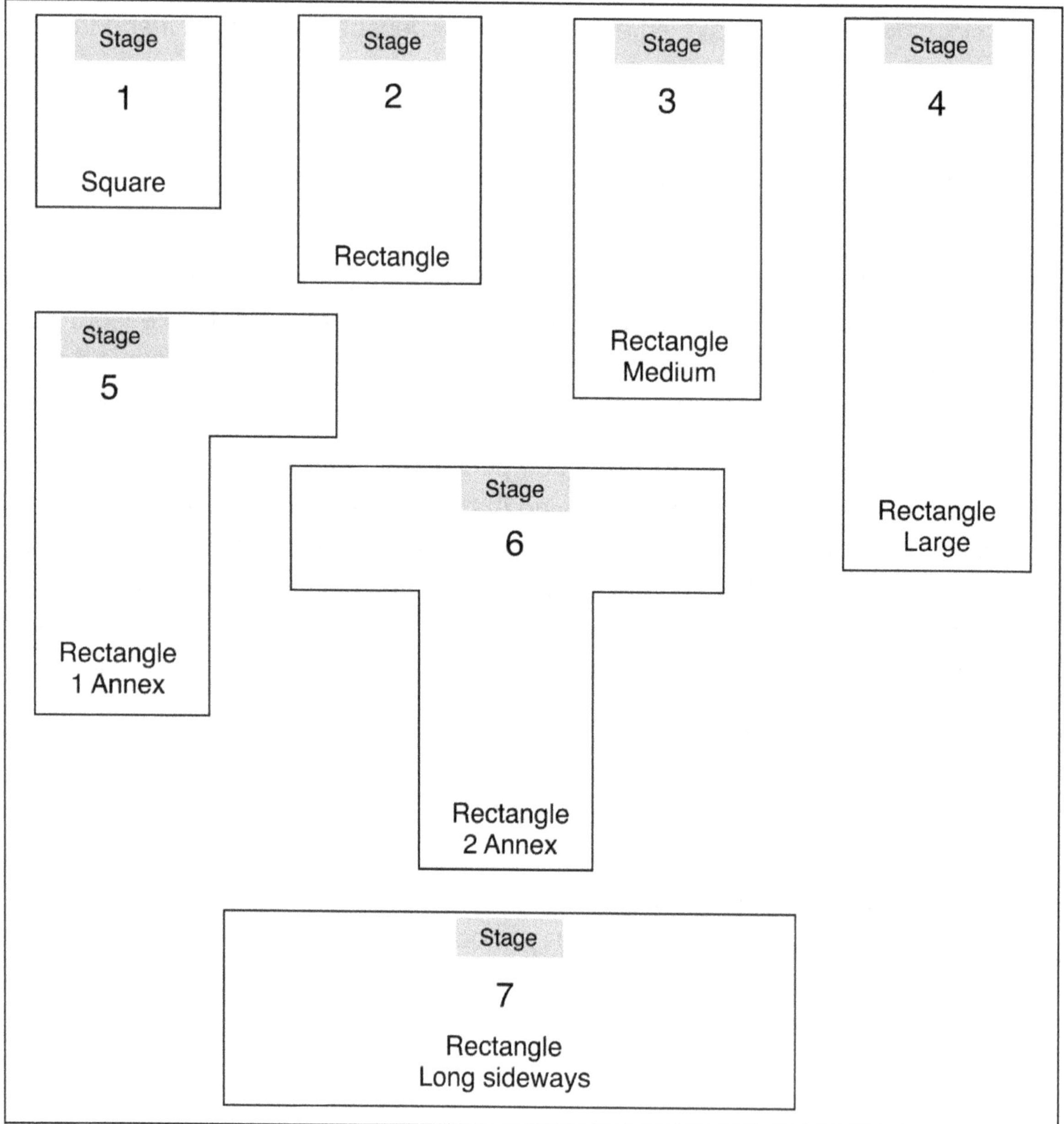



*Figure 5.1*

<u>Location</u>

Once the type of premises has been identified, the next thing to consider is the location of the following:

- Musicians
- Singers
- Computer to project video with audio
- How people are located (i.e. in cases of premises with multiple uses)
- Space for speakers
- Location of audio cables and electrical wires
- Location for the sound mixer

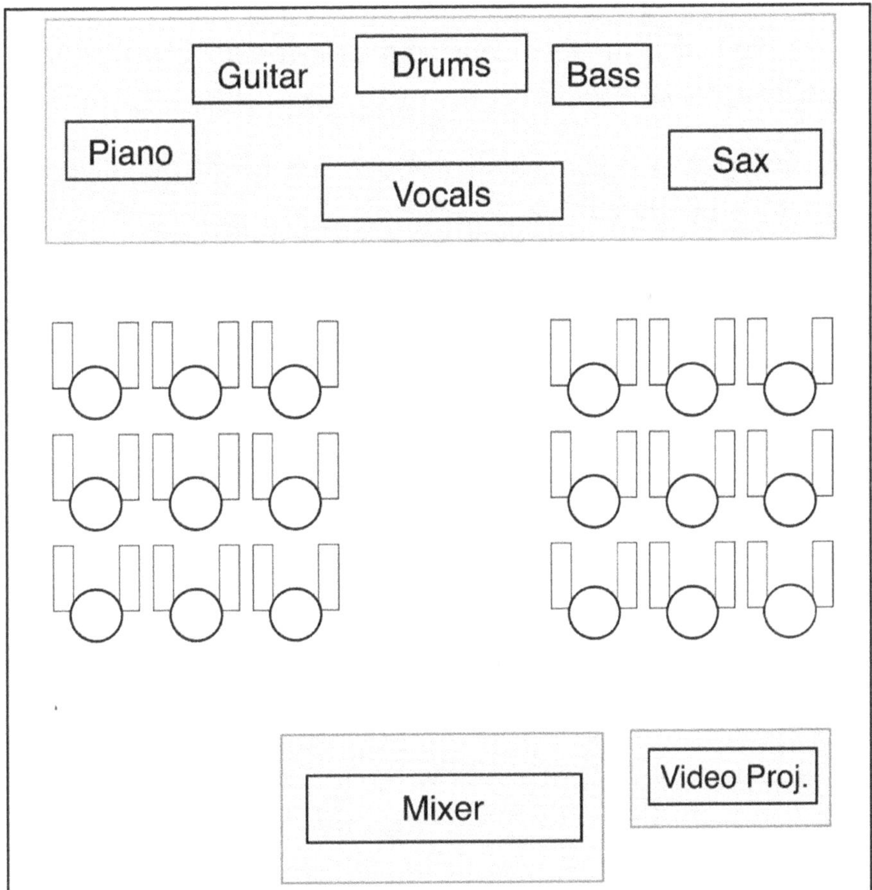


*Figure 5.2*

**Important:  The mixer must be in front or accross the main speaker to have a direct reference of the sound mixing that we are doing.**

# Chapter 6:  Acoustic of the Structure

One of the main problems that we encounter when installing or managing a sound system, is the desing and structure of the place.

The materials used for the construction of the building, the height, the size and the coating or insulation of walls, ceiling and floor, if any, will affect the sound directly. The structures are generally built of concrete, brick, wood and metal.  Some structures are covered with drywall "gibson board", others with a sound absorption material and others do not have any sound absorbing material.

How important is this?  Some believe that a sound system helps to improve the acoustic condition of the premises, but this is not true.  In an audio system, the speakers are the elastic medium causing the movement of the air molecules, and thus producing different sound waves.

When we generate some kind of sound, this will be perceived in two ways: direct and indirect sound (Figure 6.1).

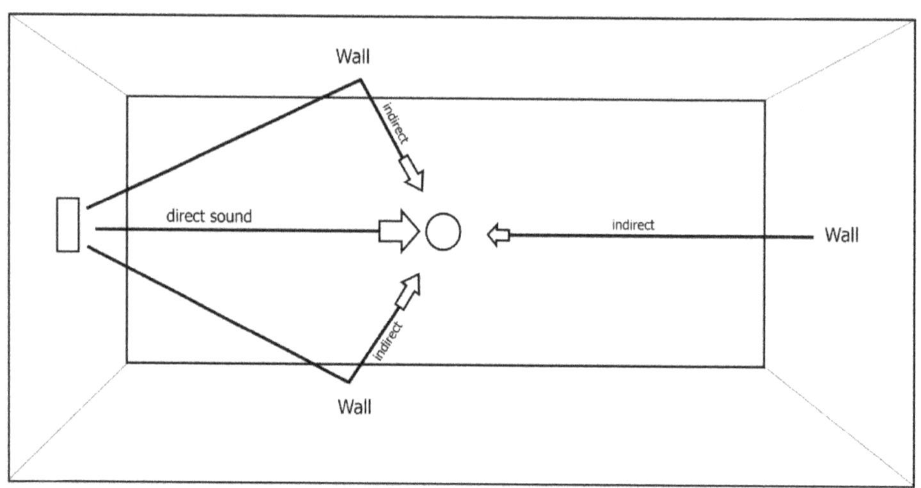


Figure 6.1

**Direct sound:** the sound that we hear, which is produced by the speakers.

**Indirect sound:** the sound that we hear as a result of a reflection in the ceiling, walls and floor of the room.

Depending on how the walls of the room are covered, it will affect the reference of the sound that the public will perceive.  When the sound wave reaches the wall, a reflection occurs.

## Reverberation

The term reflection refers to the contact of the wave with a surface, wall, floor or ceiling, and generates a repetition or copy of the wave on a smaller scale or with lower intensity.  In each reflection, part of the sound is absorbed by the surface and the other part is reflected (Figure 6.2).

This repetition is known as reverberation (reverb).  The term reverberation is the reflection that a sound has on a surface.  When a new reflection or copy of the sound comes up on the surface, it travels in the space of the room, to meet another surface, and generating another repetition.  This will occur repeatedly until it is absorbed in its entirely.

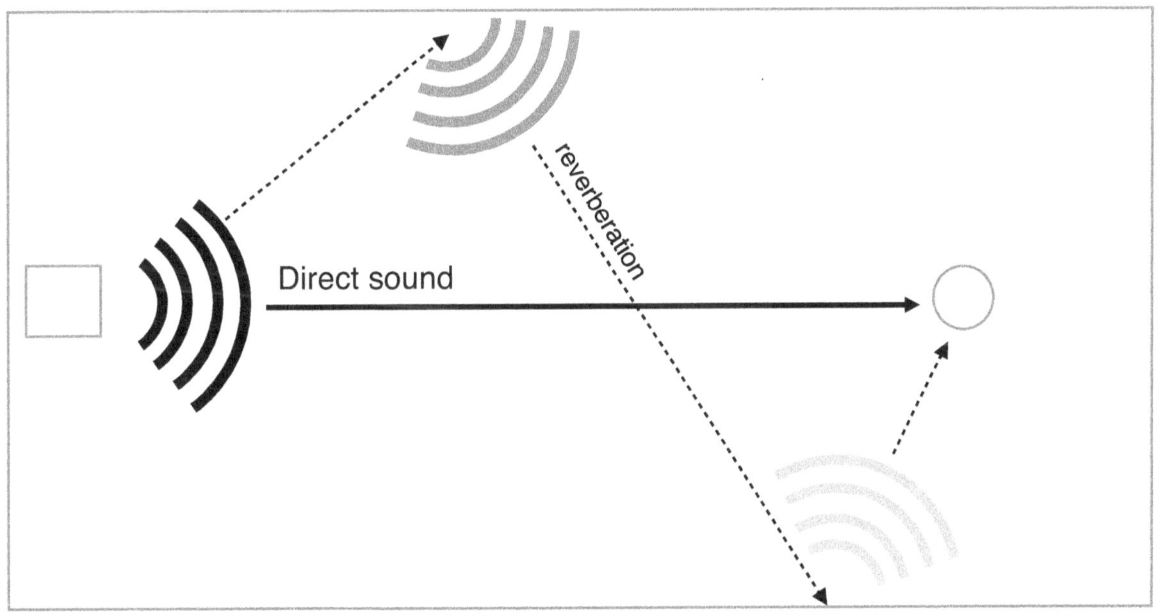


*Figure 6.2*

**Important:  *Any surface absorbs some of the sound. The absorption capacity will be primarily due to the material used in walls, floor and ceiling, and its architectural design. The architectonic design refers to the way that was planned, designed or drawn and finally the way the structure was built.***

<u>Echo</u>

When we have a **single reflection** on a surface, and it returns to the source of origin as a repetition of the sound generated, but with less intensity, it is known as echo.  To generate the echo, there must be a relation in **distance** between the source and the surface where the reflection occurs, and at the same time it will take a **period of time** until the sound generated by the surface returns to the source of origin.

The ceiling of an indoor court, for example, is usually of metal and when we use a sound system, the echo generated distorts everything that is being amplified in the activity, and is perceived as a noise.  Thus, if we have a sound that is produced **indirectly**, it is important to work with the structure of the location to avoid the rebounds on the ceiling, walls and floor.

**Important:**  *The audio system does not improve the acoustic behavior of a structure.*


<u>Scale of sound absorption</u>

All objects have the capability to bounce or absorb the sound.  This is known as *acoustic absorption capacity*.  For example, the absorptive capacity of the concrete is not the same as the absorption capacity of the carpet.  The materials have a degree of sound isolation and it is called acoustic *reflection or absorption.*

In order to know the absorption capacity of the materials you can use a scale from 0 to 1, according to the ASTM C 423 standard (Figure 6.3), which is the standard method to evaluate the absorption of noise and noise absorption coefficients based on the method of reverberation of the site.

In the graph (Figure 6.3), we see a curve depending on the frequency and absorptive capacity of the material.

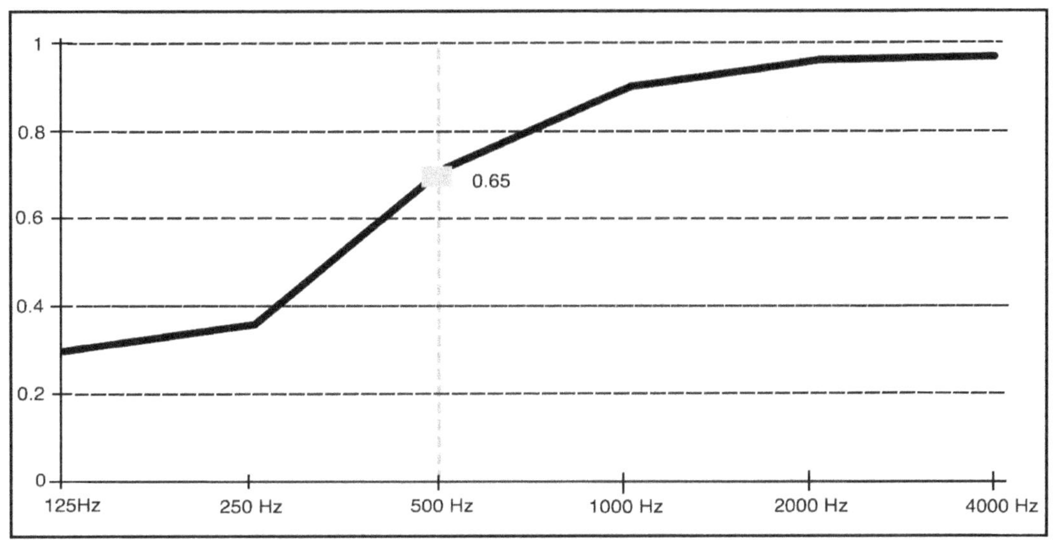


*Figure 6.3*

The information we get from the graph shows this material:

1. At 125Hz, has an absorption of 0.30 - absorbent
2. At 250 Hz, has an absorption of 0.38 - absorbent
3. At 500 Hz, has an absorption of 0.70 - very absorbent
4. At 1000Hz, has an absorption of 0.90 - extremely absorbent
5. At 2000Hz and 4000Hz, have an absorption of 0.98 – extremely absorbent

Using this scale (Figure 6.3), see the values that guide us to choose the appropriate materials according to the absorption coefficient (Figure 6.4).

A. values of 0.05, 0.10: reflective
B. values of 0.15, 0.20, 0.25: little absorbent
C. values of 0.30, 0.35, 0.40, 0.45, 0.50, 0.55: absorbent
D. values of 0.60, 0.65, 0.70 and 0.75: highly absorbent
E. values of 0.80, 0.85: Extremely absorbent
F. values of 0.90, 0.95 and 1: extremely absorbent

| Reflective | Less Absorbent | Absorbent | Highly Absorbent | Extremely Absorbent |
|---|---|---|---|---|
| 0.05 - 0.10 | 0.15 - 0.25 | 0.30 - 0.55 | 0.60 - 0.75 | 0.80 - 1 |

*Figure 6.4*

The following table will give some examples of absorption coefficient for various materials according to frequency.

| Material | Absorption coefficient depending on the frequency | | | | | |
|---|---|---|---|---|---|---|
| | 125 | 250 | 500 | 1,000 | 2,000 | 4,000 |
| Painted concrete | 0.01 | 0.01 | 0.02 | 0.02 | 0.02 | 0.04 |
| Exposed painted brick | 0.01 | 0.01 | 0.02 | 0.02 | 0.02 | 0.02 |
| Plasterboard ½" | 0.29 | 0.10 | 0.05 | 0.04 | 0.07 | 0.09 |
| Marble or tile | 0.01 | 0.01 | 0.01 | 0.01 | 0.02 | 0.02 |
| Wood board 2" from de wall | 0.30 | 0.25 | 0.20 | 0.17 | 0.15 | 0.10 |
| Rubber mat 2" | 0.04 | 0.04 | 0.08 | 0.12 | 0.03 | 0.10 |
| Polyurethane foam 1 3/8" | 0.11 | 0.14 | 0.36 | 0.82 | 0.90 | 0.97 |
| Glass wool (panel 35 kg/m) 1" | 0.20 | 0.40 | 0.80 | 0.90 | 1.00 | 1.00 |
| Glass wool (panel 35 kg/m) 2" | 0.30 | 0.75 | 1.00 | 1.00 | 1.00 | 1.00 |
| Open window | 1.00 | 1.00 | 1.00 | 1.00 | 1.00 | 1.00 |

*Figure 6.5*

# Chapter 7:  The Electric Circuit

A basic electrical circuit includes:
1. A power supply
2. Connection cables or wires
3. Electronic and electrical components that utilize part of the power

## Voltage, current and resistance

The tension generated by the power supply is known as **voltage**.  An electrical charge that travels by cable or a conductor is known as a **current**, and each component will consume part of the power, which is known as **resistance**.

1. The unit of measurement for the voltage is the volt (V).
2. The unit used in the current is the ampere (A).
3. Their resistance is expressed in units of ohms ($\Omega$).
4. The unit used to indicate power consumption is the watts (watts).

The units of measurement used to express smaller values are:

1. Millivolts (mV)
2. Milliamps (mA)
3. Kiloohms (K$\Omega$)

## Main power supply

We receive power from a main source, normally from a city electrical service, which will provide our location with an electrical connection, according to the power that we are going to use.

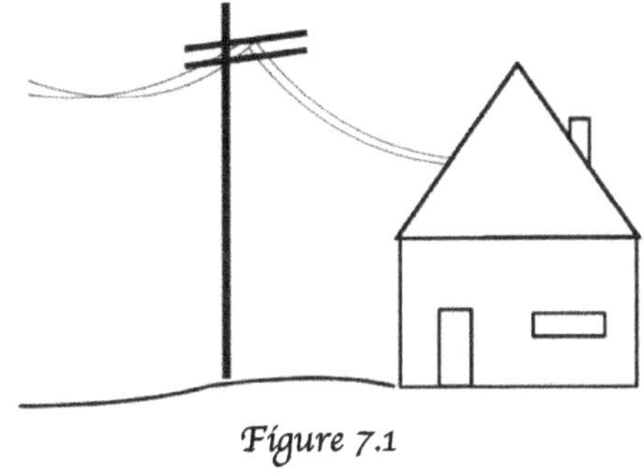

*Figure 7.1*

A house normally receives three wires.  Two cables holding 120 volts, giving us a total connection of 240 volts, and with one wire being used as a neutral charge. Larger structures with higher energy consumption are provided with a connection of three phases, known as the three-phase connection.

The wires are connected to a main electrical distribution box divided into electrical circuits (Figure 7.2).

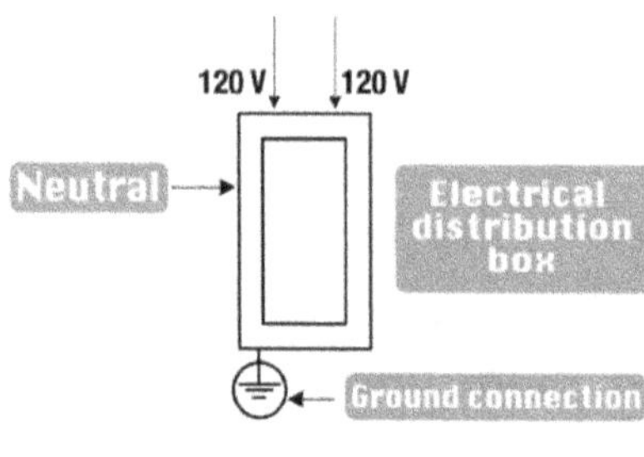


*Figure 7.2*

Some circuits will send energy to lights, receptacles, refrigerators, ovens, water heaters, etc.  The majority of circuits will send 120 V and others will send 220 V, depending on the equipment connected to the circuit, such as an electric stove.

## The ground

The main electrical box of each site is connected to a principal ground.  This is done through the installation of a solid copper rod buried in the ground (Figure 7.3).

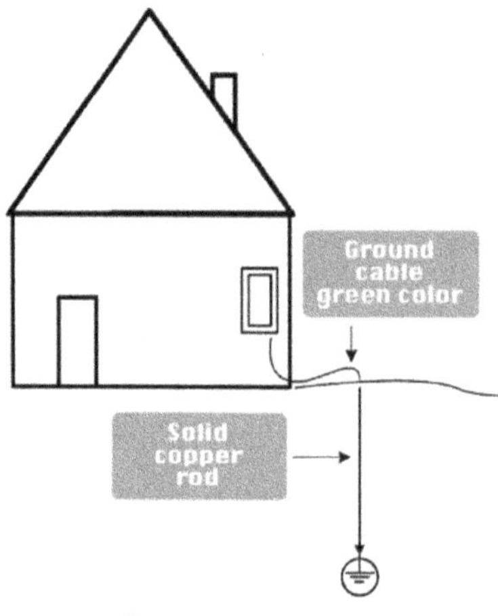


*Figure 7.3*

A cable is connected to a copper rod that leads to a bar in the electrical panel. The purpose of the bar in the panel is to connect all the ground of the circuits. Each circuit has a ground cable.

As standard, green cable is used for ground connection, and its symbol is shown in (Figure 7.4).

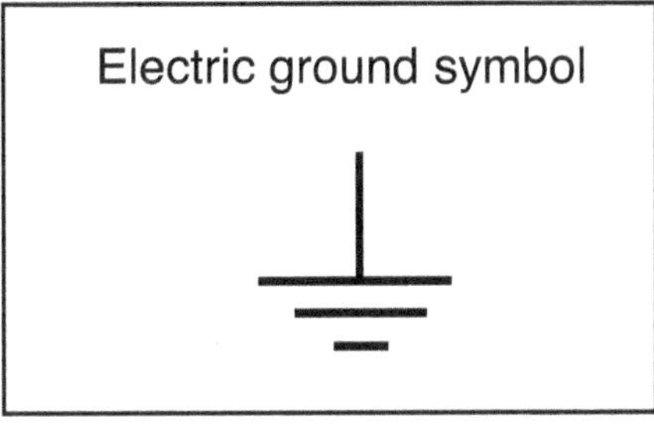


Figure 7.4

## The maximum current

The current consumption in a household is calculated by taking all electrical equipments that are being used into consideration. With this information we can determine the total capacity of current consumption. For example, a house usually has a current consumption not exceeding 100 amps (100A). Consumption of amperage will depend on the equipment connected in the electrical circuits.

The electrical circuits can be distributed to:

1. Bulbs and receptacles
2. Refrigerator
3. Electric ovens
4. Electric stoves
5. Water heaters
6. Air conditioning
7. Heating

<u>Current consumption</u>

After the distribution of our main electrical system into the circuits, we will begin to connect electrical and electronic components.  All cables and connected equipment will consume part of the current that travels through each circuit.

All in all, we have a power supply **voltage**, a line of distribution where the **current** will travel, and consumption of equipment that have a **resistance**.

Make a list of your equipment and calculate the total consumption.  The electrical unit ***watts*** are used to indicate the power consumption of a given device.  That information it is provided in the back of the gear, or consult the operator manual.

Use the following formula to make the calculation of consumption (Figure 7.5).

W = Watts, A = Ampere, V = Volt

1.  To calculate Watts (W = A x V)
2.  To calculate Ampere (A = W ÷ V)
3.  To calculate Volt (V = W ÷ A)

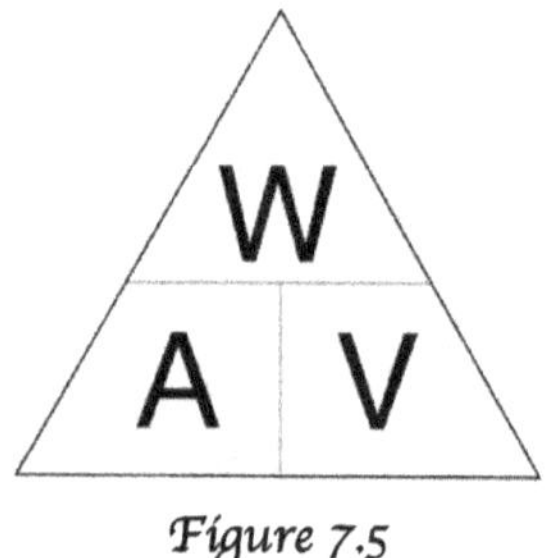


*Figure 7.5*

Example:

You have sound system wich the total sum is 3,800 watts.  As we mentioned before, the voltage in a regular circuit it is normally 120 volts and the ampere is 20 amps for each circuit.  To know the total amperage and how many circuits your sound system need, use the following formula:

A = W ÷ V

A = 3,800 watts ÷ 120 volts

A = 32 amps

With that result, you need at least 2 circuit of 20 amps.

Important:  For safety and prevent overheating in the circuit, use an 80% of consumption of the total ampere in each circuit.  For example, a circuit with 20 amps in total, the 80% is 16 amps.

# Chapter 8:  The Ground Loop

Our audio system, such as the equipment used in the stage, will use the local power supply.  It should be a secure and independent power.  When we talk about independent, we refer to a connection that is not connected to other electrical circuits, such as lights, air conditioning, kitchen equipment, lights effects on stage, and any other connection that may cause interference to the equipment.

***The equipment used in the stage, and all additional equipment connected to the sound system, should be electrically powered from the same socket of the main audio system.***

Here is an example of a power supply with two electric circuits.

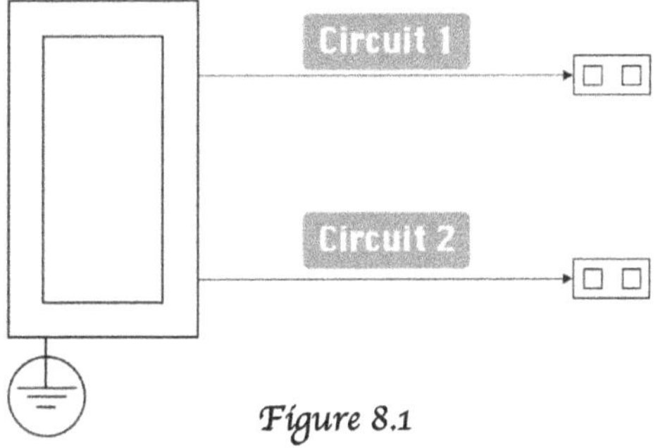


*Figure 8.1*

When we connect our sound system to one of the circuits, we have a ground connection without interference and without the likelihood of noise in our system.

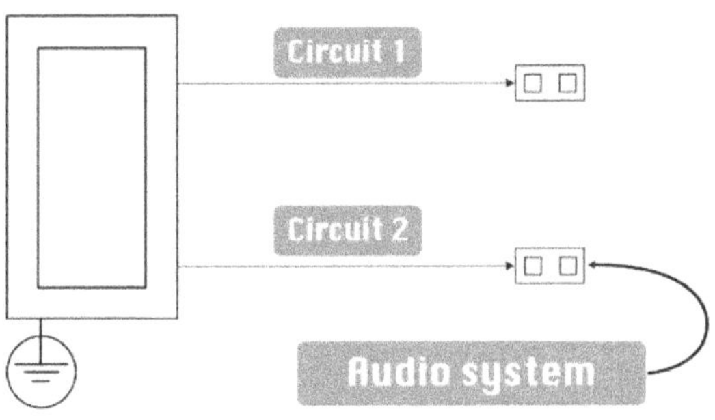


*Figure 8.2*

# ¿What happens if we connect the audio system to different circuits?

The problem of connecting to audio system to different circuits is the probability of making a bridge between the ground of circuit one and the ground of circuit two. This causes an interconnection between cables of ground forming what is known as the **ground loop**.

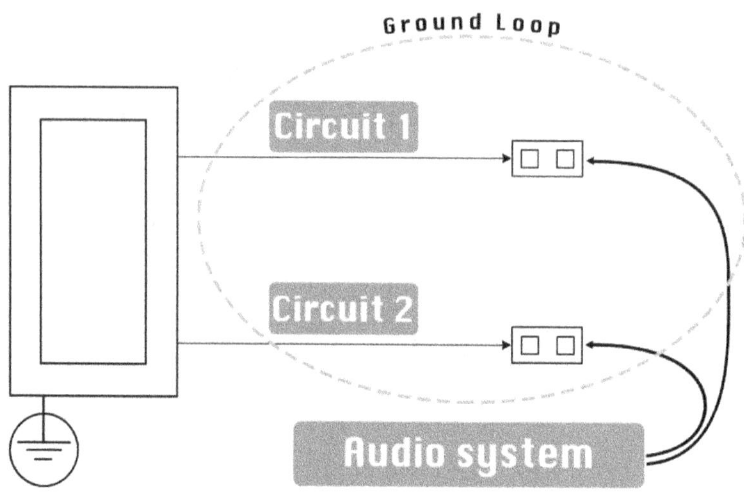


*Figure 8.3*

The **ground loop** occurs when the ground of the circuits is interconnected, forming a circle or loop all over the place, leaving our system in the middle (Figure 8.4).

At the same time, this connection receives a small voltage supply, which is captured as interference by the audio system.

This interference is perceived as noise in the electronic equipment. When you install a sound system the interference is amplified, causing a buzz or an unwanted hum in our loudspeakers.

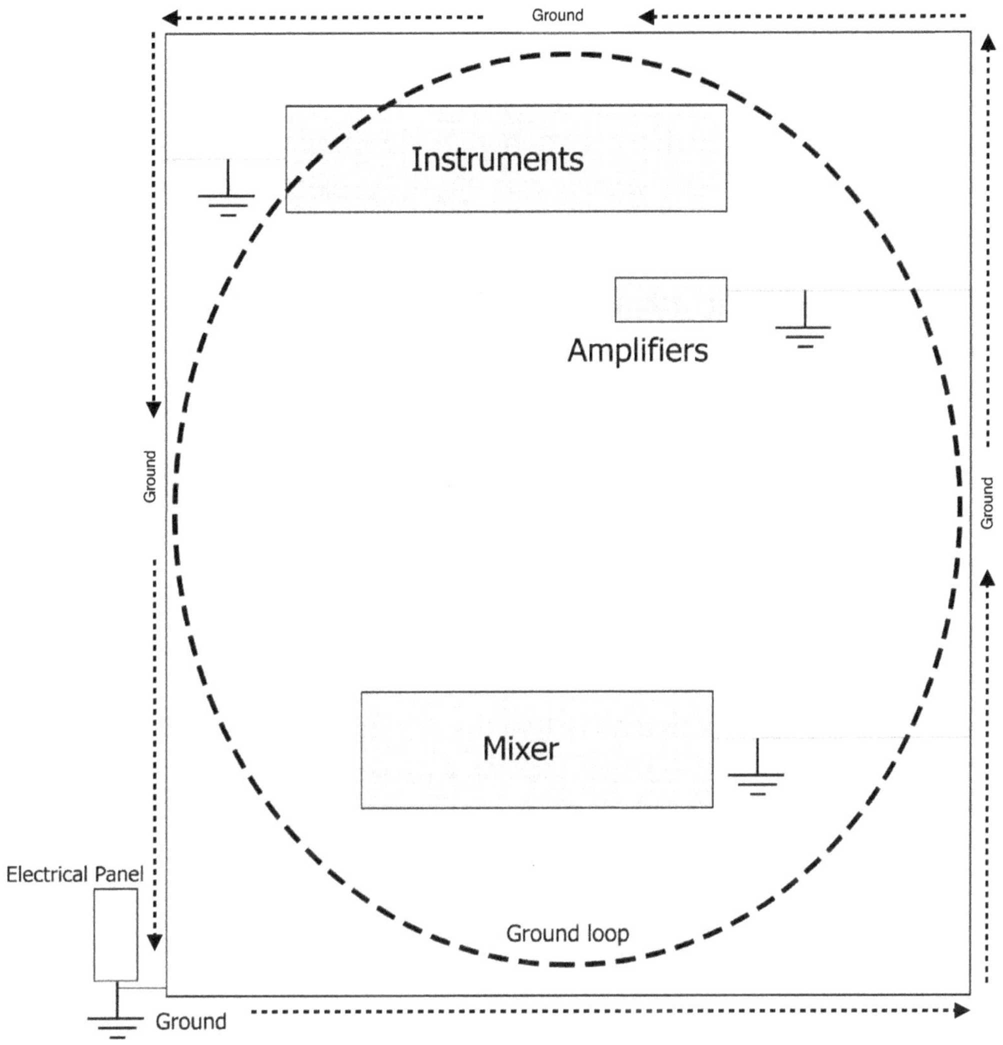



*Figure 8.4*
*Equipment connected to different circuits*
*causing a "ground loop" in the audio system*

# Chapter 9:  Electrical Charge

Knowing how much electric charge our sound equipment requires, is vital for its optimal operation.  Equipment with a low capacity electrical charge will cause a deficiency in each component of our audio system.

***The efficiency of the equipment will depend, at first, of a good electrical connection.***

In addition, the type of cable used to carry the current to each equipment is crucial.  Of course, we could use any electrical cable to turn on an equipment, but this doesn't mean that it will work efficiently.

The electrical cables come in different thicknesses, and are numbered depending on the thickness.  The higher the number, the thinner the cable.  The smaller the number, the thicker the cable.  The length of the cable will also play an important factor.  The issue with longer cables is that the temperature in the cable rises, which causes a loss of current.  If we use incorrect cables for electrical connection, our equipment can be on and running, but not working at its full capacity.

Factors that indicate a loss of current are:
1. distortion in the audio of the speakers
2. power loss

If we have any lamp connected to the audio system, we will see how the light gets dimmer as there is more demand of power in the system.

The following guidelines will help maintain the proper current connections, but **first speak with a professional in the electrical field so that he can help you to configure the system.**

## Basic guide for a permanent connection

- Determine the electrical charge of the equipment.  This will help you know the capacity of the main breaker that you are using and how many circuits you need. (View Chapter 7:  Current consumption)
- Install a sub panel connected to the main breaker, which you will use to distribute the circuits of the sound system.
- Install a separate ground connection appart from ground connection of the venue.
- The console, amplifiers and the equipment used on stage will be connected to the same electrical sub panel.  In other words, the sound system as well as everything connected on the stage, such as instrument's amplifiers, synthesizers, etc., are connected to the same electrical panel determined for the sound.
- Distribute the circuits for the console, speaker's amplifiers, digital processors, projection, stage, and instruments.

## Basic guide for a mobile connection

- Determine the electrical charge of the equipment.  (View Chapter 7:  Current consumption)
- Install a connection to the main panel of the venue using a three-conductor cable for 120 volts or four-conductor for 220 volts, depending on the equipment capacity.
    - 120 volts wire connection:  black (hot or power), white (neutral), green (ground)
    - 220 volts wire connection:  2 black (hot or power), white (neutral), green (ground)
- Prepare the main outlet panel from which the current will be distributed to the equipment.  Each outlet circuit with 20 amps breaker and 12 awg wire cable.
- Make sure that the thickness and the length of the extensions are appropriate for the current consumption of the equipment.
- The current used for the mixer will be the same as the equipment used on the stage. This means that all are connected to the same electrical panel determined for the gear.

# Chapter 10: Audio and Signal Cables

The interconnection of our equipment, which includes the mixer, amplifiers, processors, speakers, microphones and instruments, will be done by using different types of cables according to the required application. A basic example: a microphone cable is not the same cable that we use for a guitar. The construction of each cable is different, because they are made for different uses.

**Note**: *Today, with the increase in technology, the connection between equipments is extensive and the same type of cable can be used for various applications.*

Before discussing the types of cables, the following chart (Figure 10.1), will show different thicknesses of wires and its application. To find out the cable thickness, we use the AWG (American Wire Gauge) abbreviation. Remember that the higher the number, the thinner the cable.

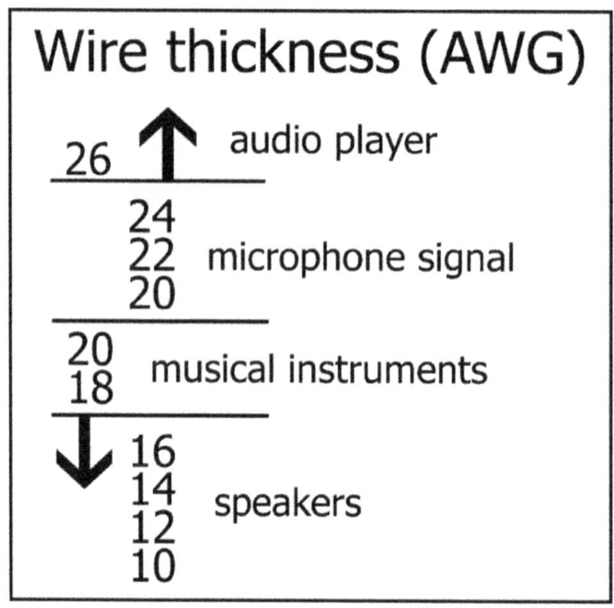


*Figure 10.1*

# Length of the speaker cords

The lenght of the cables is an important factor when installing the system. A longer cable will cause a voltage drop and a current loss due to the resistance that the cable have to manage. The thicker the wire, the less resistance will exert and therefore a stronger passage of current.

The cables to connect to the speakers will go from the amplifiers to the speakers. The function of the amplifiers is to send the amplified signal to the speakers through the current that travels along the wire that we use. Depending on the venue, the amplifiers may be at a distance of 25, 50, 75 and up to 100 feet. This is important, because the cable that we will use depends on the distance between the speakers and the equipment. Consider the following chart (Figure 10.2).

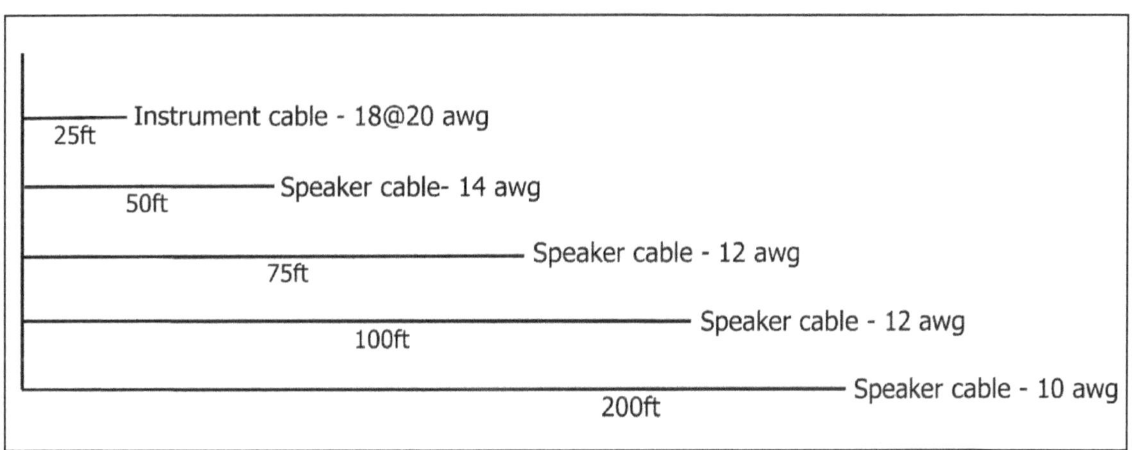


*Figure 10.2*

# Difference between unbalanced and balanced cable

The use of appropriate cables is very important, because this will directly affect the sound quality of the system. Each cable in an audio system has the potential to add noise and compromises the sound quality in the system; therefore, it is imperative to use the right cable for the right application.

## Unbalanced cable (Mono)

The unbalanced cable consists of two connectors and two conductors.  One of the conductors, which is in the center, is the signal cable, and the other conductor surrounding the main cable, goes to the ground.

The ground connection has two functions:
1.  It charges part of the audio signal
2.  It works as a **shield** to prevent external interference of noise, which could enter to the main signal.  It has the function of rejecting noise, but when the distance from the cable is long, the ground conductor can act as a receiver and add noise to the signal (Figure 10.3).

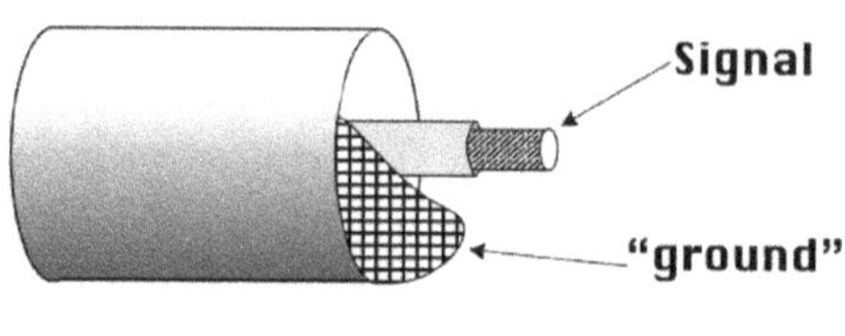


*Figure 10.3*

Unbalanced cables work well with musical instruments that are connected to amplifiers with no more than 15 to 20 feet length.

## Balanced cable (Canon)

The balanced cable has three conductors.  Two conductors charge the signal and the other is the ground connection. The three conductors are twisted, thus exerting a shield against noise.  In addition, many times this cable has inside an aluminum coating to protect it even more from interference (Figure10.4).

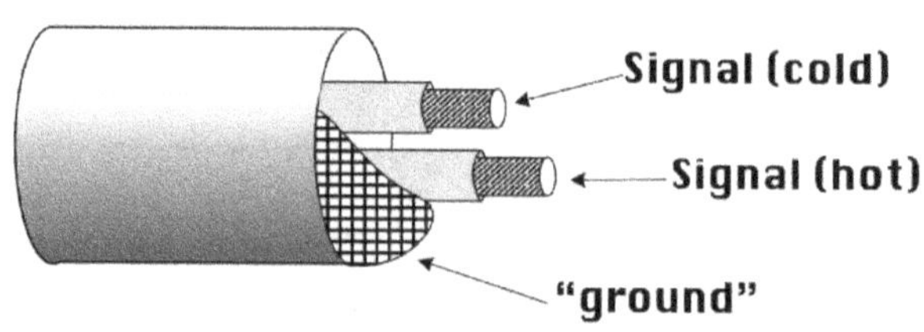


*Figure 10.4*

# Chapter 11: Connectors

## Audio player connector with 26 awg cable upward

(Example: CD player, iPod, computer, etc.)

- Stereo connector (Figure 11.1) - It has 3 conductors where we will get a left channel, a right channel and a ground connection.

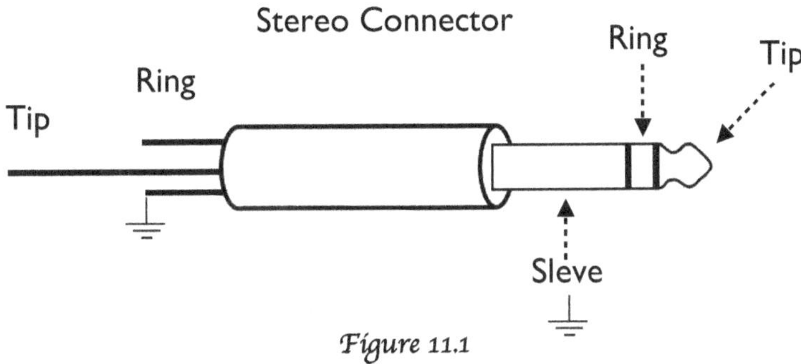



*Figure 11.1*

## Microphone and signal connector with 24-20 awg cable

- XLR connector (Figure 11.2) - It has 3 conductors and is known as a balanced connector (canon).  Very used for its ability to avoid interference.

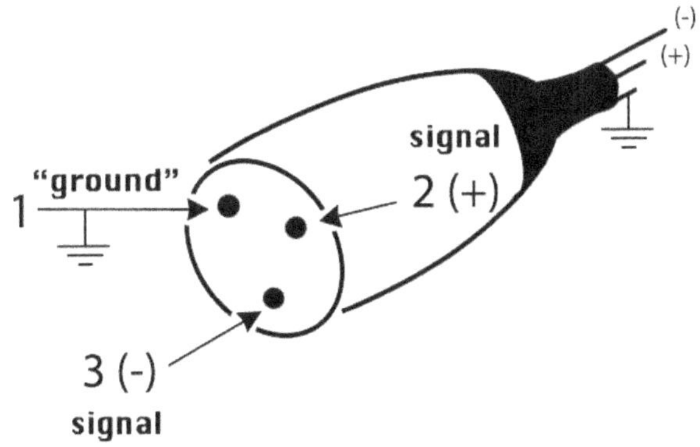



*Figure 11.2*

<u>Unbalanced signal connector with 20-18 awg cable</u>

* Mono connector (Figure 11.3) - Also known as 1/4 cable.  It has 2 conductors and is used in musical instruments like the guitar, the electric piano, the bass, etc.
* When using the 1/4 cable as a signal cable, that is, to send the audio from one device to another, consider that it only has 2 cables, which makes it unbalanced. For longer distances, will add interference and noise to the equipment.

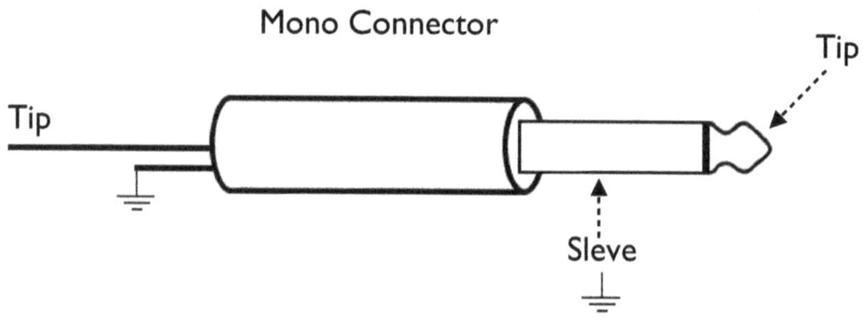


*Figure 11.3*

<u>Speaker and monitor connector with 16-10 awg cable</u>

* Mono connector (Figure 11.3) - Used in passive speakers.  Passive speakers are speakers that do not have amplification in their own box.

* SpeakON connector (Figure 11.4) - This connector is widely used in passive speakers and amplifiers.  Depending on the application and configuration of the speakers, it comes to be used with 2, 4 and 8 conductor cables.  This connector also has a lock that prevents it from being easily disconnected, providing security in the connection. (Images of Neutrik connectors are used with permission).

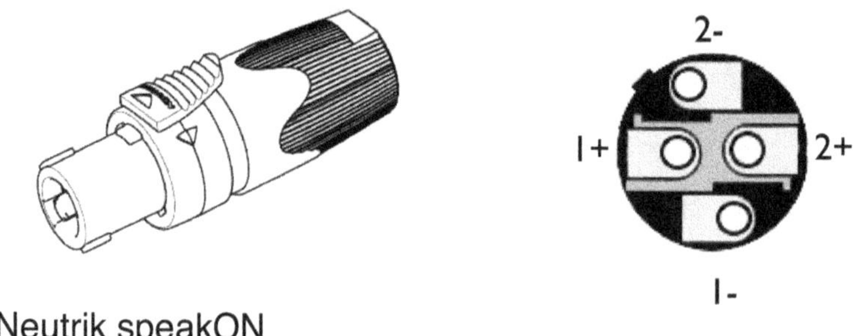


Neutrik speakON

*Figure 11.4*

# Chapter 12: The Speaker

If we analyze an audio system, we will find that the speakers occupy the last place in the amplification chain of an audio signal (Figure 12.1).

At the same time, they will be responsible for projecting the amplified sound to the audience after going through all the electrical processing. The speaker is a type of **transducer** that convert the electrical signal (electrical energy) received from the amplifiers to an acoustical energy.

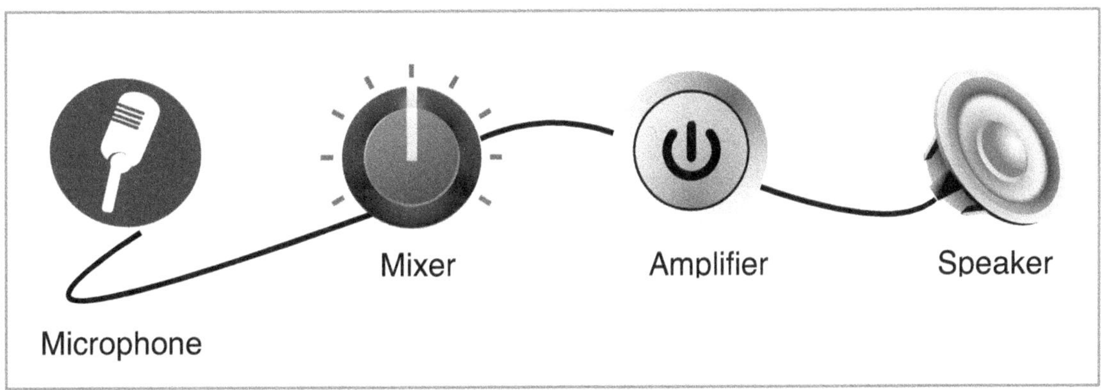


*Figure 12.1*

The role played by the speaker is of the utmost importance, since the audience that will be present, even though they do not know how to work with an audio system, they already have a very personal reference. This is because of how the music industry has evolved.

The design of audio equipment in automobiles, hearing aids, radios, home theater systems, mp3, ipod and many more are studied and designed so that the consumer has a pleasant experience with what he listens to.

What does this have to do with the audio system? It has much to do. To design these equipment, it has had to take the following considerations:

- acoustic elements
- frequencies
- space of sound dispersion
- mixing and mastering the audio
- location of the receiver in case of cars and home theaters systems

As we see, there is science and engineering behind all equipment design for personal consumption, thus providing a good sound quality.

The study and design of the audio system is prepared with the aim that the listener has a legitimate reference of the original sound that will be reproduced, in this case, by the speaker.

## Types of speaker

The speakers are divided into two groups: those with an amplifier in their own acoustic box will be called **active** speaker, and those with the amplifier as external source will be called **passive** speaker (Figure 12.2).

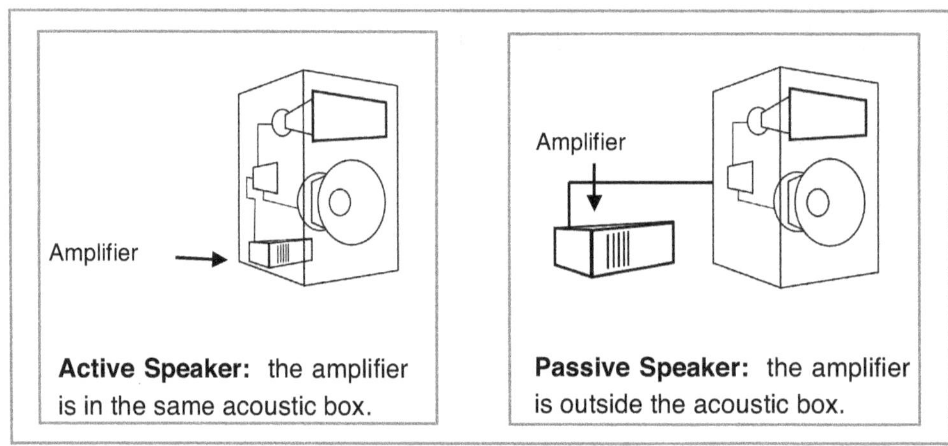


*Figure 12.2*

## Parts of the speaker (Figure 12.3)

1. **The acoustic box:** is designed in order to maximize sound reproduction of low, medium and high frequencies, depending on the application. It is made of wood, pressed wood and plastic.
2. **The tweeter:** it is a transducer designed for reproduction of high-pitched sounds.
3. **The woofer:** it is a transducer used for the reproduction of medium and low frequencies.
4. **The crossover:** the frequency divider filter. It is responsible of sending high frequencies to the "tweeter", and medium and low frequencies to the "woofer".
5. **The baffle:** opening that allows the sound wave to come out of the back.

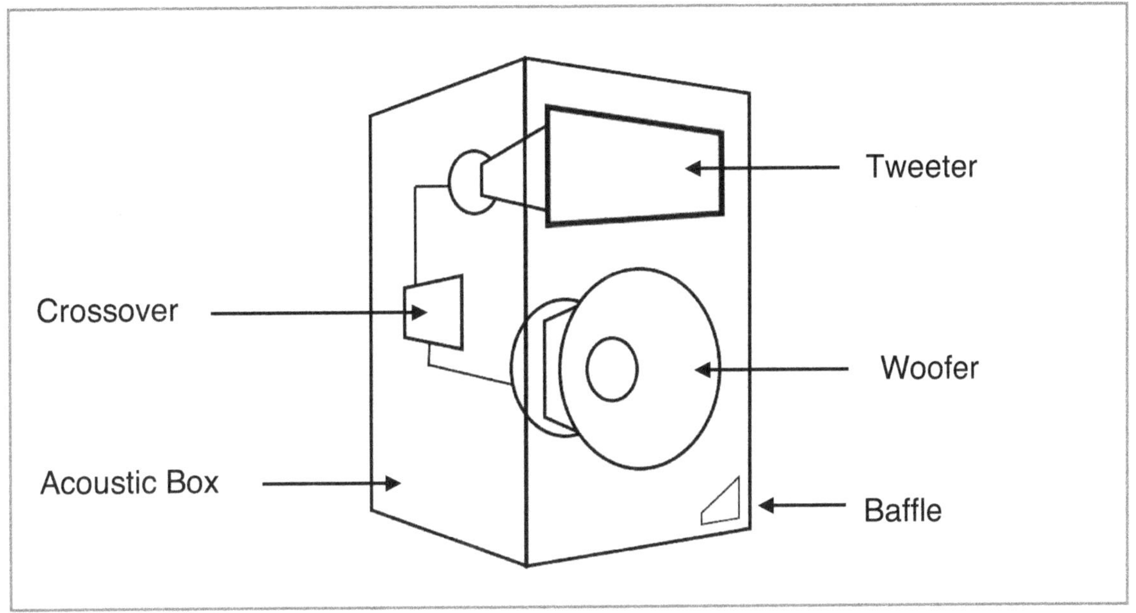


*Figure 12.3*

# Chapter 13:  Types of Speakers

## Low frequency speakers

- **The sub bass** (Figure 13.1)

<u>Main features:</u>

1.  It is a loudspeaker designed primarily for low frequency reproduction
2.  Used for frequency range between 20Hz and 250Hz
3.  They are usually located on the ground
4.  Their coverage is omnidirectional

*Omnidirectional coverage* means that the sound is propagated in all directions.  The sound pressure is higher in the area where the woofer is located; however, the sound emitted by the sub bass will propagate equally in all directions with lower intensity.  We could have problems with some sub bass frequency, depending on its location.

**Important:** *Passive sub basses do not come with a crossover or crossover filter inside.  We must install one, either analog or digital, in order to choose the appropriate frequency cut-off.*

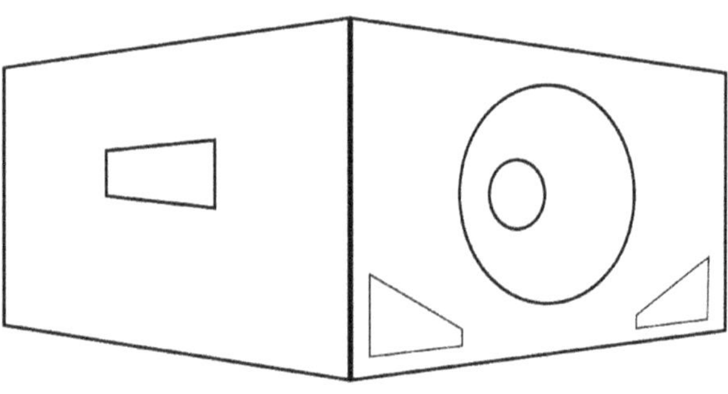

*Figure 13.1*

<u>Full range speaker</u> (Figure 13.2)

The full range speaker design consists of a woofer speaker, for low and medium frequencies, and a high frequency speaker known as tweeter.

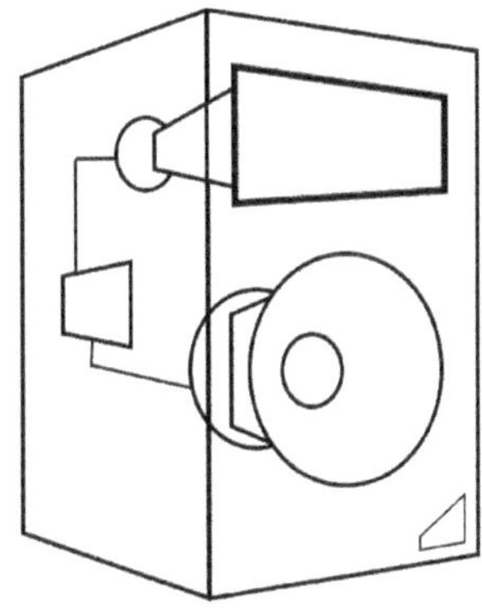

*Figure 13.2*

<u>Main features:</u>

1.  The woofer will reproduce the low and mid frequencies, usually between 45Hz y 1.5kHz
2.  The tweeter will reproduce high frequencies between 1.5kHz y 20kHz
3.  They can be active or passive
4.  They contain a frequency divider filter. It should be noted that the woofer is capable of reproducing some high frequencies and the tweeter can reproduce some average frequencies. This being so, frequency cancellations will occur, causing a poor reproduction of the sound and the listener will not perceive some frequencies. To avoid this, a frequency divider or crossover is used.

## The crossover

Each speaker has a crossover inside. The crossover is an electronic piece whose main function is to avoid that frequencies of the woofer mix with those of the tweeter, and vice versa. By means of a study of measurement, the frequency in which both are crossed, the woofer and the tweeter is determined, and attenuate in that point with the crossover, avoiding cancellation of frequencies. It is a complete study of operation and application, and if we take these principles, we must evaluate the **technical aspects of the speaker**.

# Chapter 14: Technical Aspects of the Speaker

A. Coverage
B. Wattage
C. Sensitivity
D. Impedance (resistance in ohms)

## A. Coverage

Each speaker comes with a design that covers horizontal or vertical range (Figure 14.1).

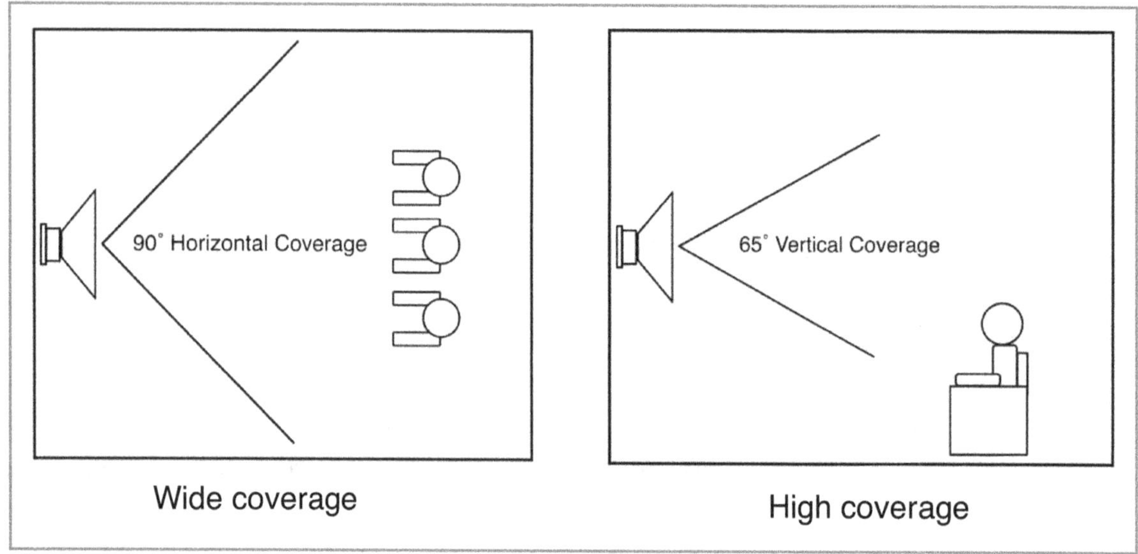


Figure 14.1

The sound is controlled in the vertical and horizontal axis. The control is measured in degrees, for example: 90° of horizontal coverage and 65° of vertical coverage.

## B. Wattage

Each speaker has a consumption of power expressed in watts. The quantity of watts in the speaker will let us know the electric power necessary to operate the speaker and this power will be applied with an amplifier.

It is important to mention that most of the power received by the speaker dissipates in a form of heat, increasing its temperature.

Many times the information that we find in the acoustic cabinet of the speaker regarding the power is divided in three:
1.  Average power (RMS)
2.  Maximum power "Program"
3.  Peak power

In Figure 14.2, using and average power (RMS) as an example, we can see the difference between the power ratings.  If the speaker has 200 "watts" RMS, then we will have the following technical information:

- 200 "watts" average power (RMS)
- 400 "watts" maximum power (Program)
- 800 "watts" peak power

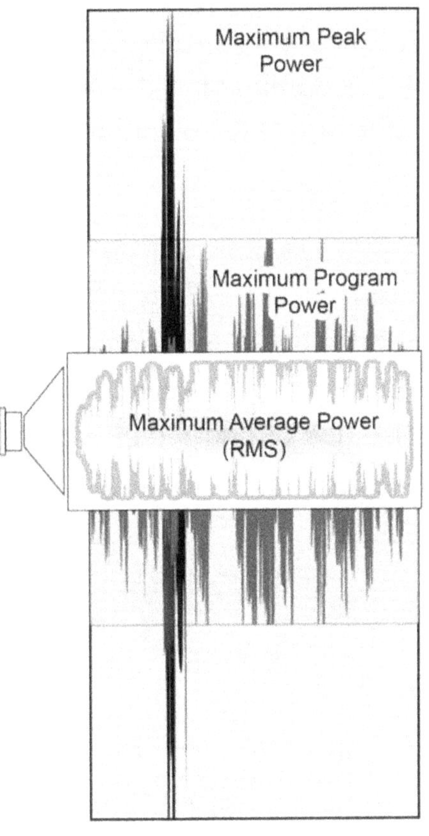


*Figure 14.2*

40

### Average power (RMS)

The average power o RMS (*root-means-square)*, is the maximum value to make sure that the speaker does not burn or overheat; therefore, it provides information about the constant power to operate the speaker safely.  For example:  200 "watts" RMS.

### Maximum power (program)

Generally, the maximum power is double the RMS power.  It is the power that reaches the microphone during the typical musical program, taking into consideration two factors: that it lasts a short period of time, and that the values of the power are considerably less than the maximum.  This power helps us when is time to make a decision with the amplifier.  Example: 400 "watts" program.

### Peak power

The peak power, is the maximum power that a speaker can manage on a certain moment, for a short period of time.  This value is related to the maximum level that the speaker may hold before it gets damaged.  If the sound signal is kept at the peak power constantly it will result in a damage to the diaphragm or cone of the speaker.  Example: 800 "watts" peak.

## C.  Sensitivity

The *sound pressure level is the level of sound pressure that can be maintained* in the acoustic box with a determined power.  It is defined as the level of sound pressure perceived at a distance of one meter when applied to an electric power of one "watt" (Figure 14.3).

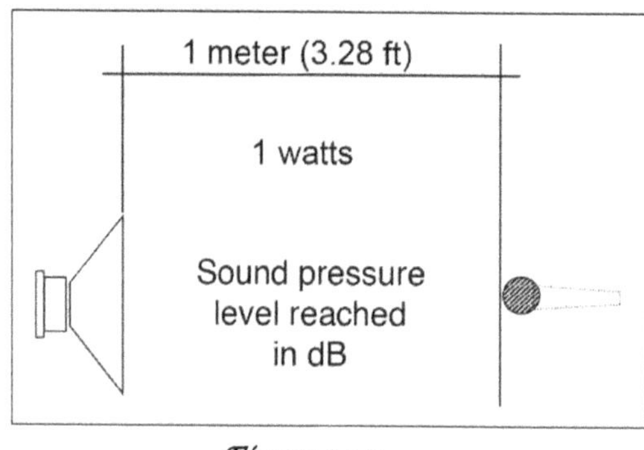


Figure 14.3

This test is performed in a room free of reflexions known as the anechoic chamber. Based on this, the sound pressure level can be determined at the same distance under any power level. The unit that we will utilize to identify the sensibility of a speaker is the decibel and its abreviation is dB.

For example, lets suppose that we have a speaker that holds 98dB of sensitivity and 400 watts of RMS power. This speaker reaches the 98 dB at one meter and a measurement of 1 watts of power was applied at the laboratory.

Utilizing the following formula, we can determine the maximum level in decibel reached by the speaker when we apply 400 watts at one meter or 3.28 feets.

$$ SPL = 10 \log_{10} \frac{400 \text{ w}}{1 \text{ w}} = 26 \text{ dB} $$

$$ SPL = 98 \text{ dB} + 26 \text{ dB} = 124 \text{ dB} $$

SPL = sound pressure level; this speaker reached 124 dB maximun of sound pressure at a distance of one meter.

## D.  Impedance of the speaker (ohms)

All the speakers have a consumption of energy equal to the resistance of an electric circuit. The resistance of the speaker or the consumption of energy will vary depending on the frequency that it is generating. In the design of the speaker, the energy consumption is determined and it will be known as the impedance of the speaker and the unit to be utilized will be the ohms which symbol is ($\Omega$).

There are speakers with impedance of 4 and 8 ohms ($\Omega$). These are the common values.

The value of power (watts) and impedance (ohms) of the speaker will be utilized to identify the best amplifier.

# Chapter 15: The Amplifier

The amplifiers can be classified in two categories. The amplifiers of low level or preamplifiers, and the power amplifiers. The **preamplifiers** are integrated to the mixing console and its finality is to bring the signals from the low level to line level. The line level signal is the one we need in the output of the mixer.

The **power amplifiers** receive the line level signal at its entrance and it amplifies it until it reaches the level of power required. The power amplifiers play an important role in the distribution chain of an audio system and it is responsible to send the amplified signal to the speakers (Figure 15.1).

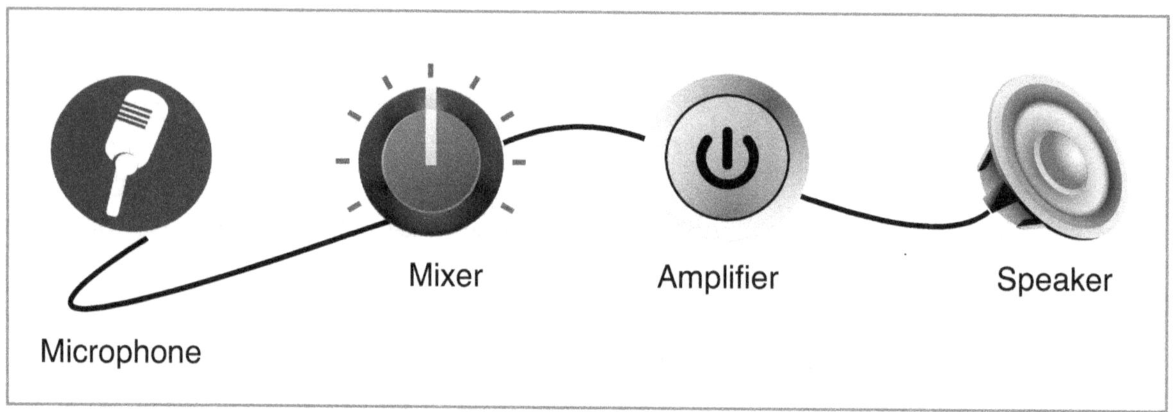


Figure 15.1

We will identify the amplifier with the following symbol.

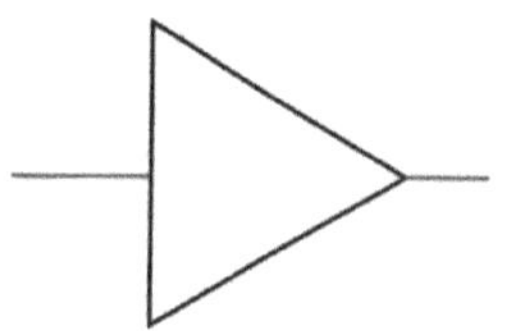

Figure 15.2

<u>Amplifier Parts</u>

The power amplifier has two channels with which we can make a stereo distribution, Left, and Right. On the front panel (Figure 15.3) we will find:

- Two buttons for volume, one for channel A and one for channel B.
- A power button.

**Note:** If the amplifier is digital, we can also find some digital processor integrated.

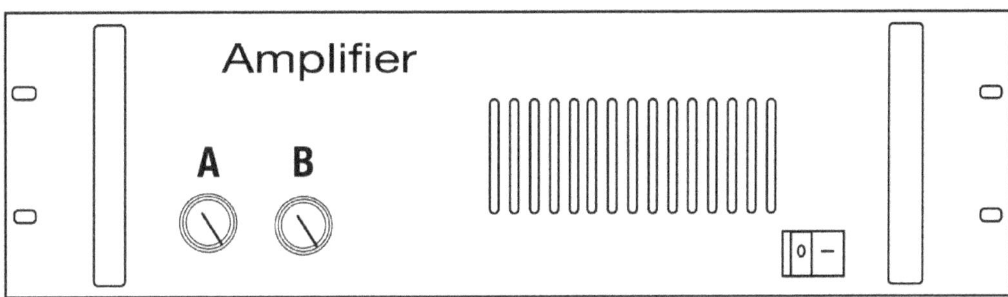


Figure 15.3

On the back panel (Figure 15.4) we will find:

<u>Inputs</u>
- Two inputs. One for channel one and the other for channel two.
- The Input connections use cables with terminals XLR or ¼ mono.
- They have a parallel connection where we can send the input signal to another amplifier.

<u>Outputs</u>
- The are two outputs. One for channel one and the other for channel two.
- The outputs can be connected with:
  - *"Speakon"* Connector
  - ¼ mono Connector
  - *"Bannana" Connection.*

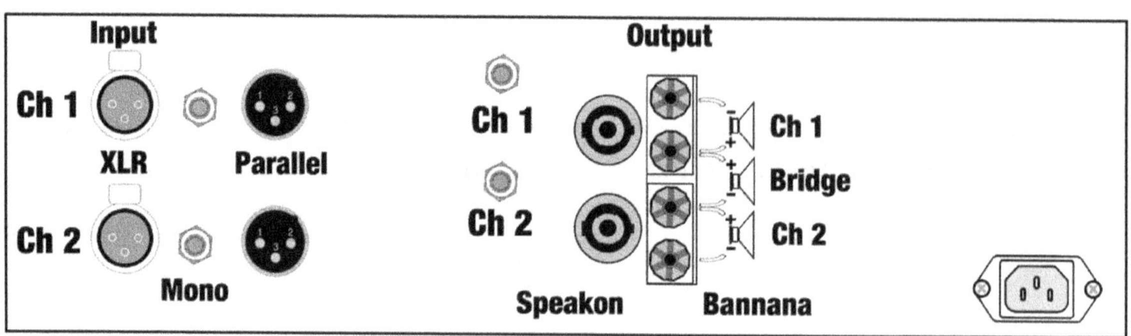


*Figure 15.4*

## Power specifications for each channel

The outputs of the amplifiers are connected to the speakers. Depending on the impedance of the speakers, there will be a response from the power amplifier. The connection between a speaker and an amplifier it is known as the impedance of charge. The power amplifier is proportional to the impedance.

A. Example: We have an amplifier in which the specifications indicate that when a speaker is connected to an impedance of 8 $\Omega$, it will generate a maximum power of 300 watts per channel. In other words, there will be 300 watts for channel one and 300 watts for channel two (Figure 15.5).

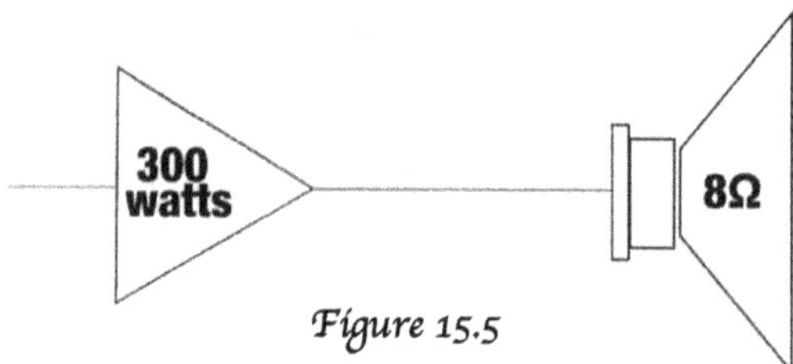


*Figure 15.5*

a. Now, the amplifier can handle several load impedances that are normally 4 $\Omega$ and 8 $\Omega$. This means that depending on the speaker impedance, it will be the output power of the amplifier. Therefore, the same amplifier of the previous example will vary its power depending on the impedance.

b. This same amplifier tells us in its specifications that when you connect a speaker with an impedance of 4 $\Omega$, it will generate a maximum power of 600 watts per channel.

Continuing from where we left off, if the impedance of the speaker is:

    i.  8 Ω, there will be 300 watts of power per channel (Figure 15.6)

  ii.  4 Ω, there will be 600 watts of power per channel (Figure 15.7)

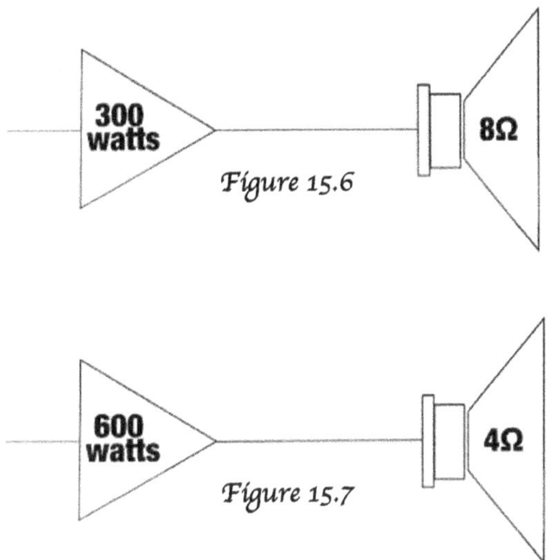


*Figure 15.6*

*Figure 15.7*

This is very important because the speakers are normally designed with impedance of 4 Ω and 8 Ω.

## Bridge connection

As we have discussed, the amplifier will generate power for each channel, but we can also obtain the sum of the power from channel one with the power of channel two. This sum is possible by making a bridge between the two channels and it is known as a **bridge connection** (Figure 15.8).

All the power from the amplifier is connected through the bridge connection. To obtain a bridge connection, you must use the banana positive (+) terminal from channel one and the banana positive (+) terminal from channel two.

The positive terminal of the speaker cable will be connected to the banana terminal of channel one, and the negative terminal of the speaker cable will be connected to the banana terminal of channel two, as shown on Figure 15.8.

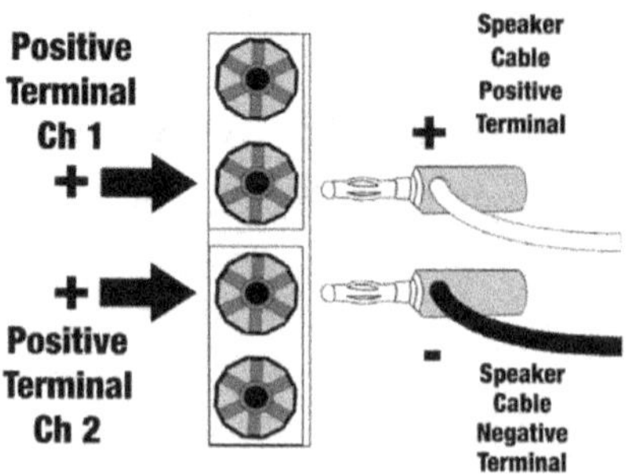


*Figure 15.8*

A bridge connection can manage an impedance charge of up to 2 Ω.  Being thus the specifications of the power of the amplifier that we have used as an example, can contain the following:

| Power specifications of the amplifier output | | |
|---|---|---|
| Channel 1 | Channel 2 | Bridge |
| | | 2 Ω / 2400 watts |
| 4 Ω / 600 watts | 4 Ω / 600 watts | 4 Ω / 1200 watts |
| 8 Ω / 300 watts | 8 Ω / 300 watts | 8 Ω /  600 watts |

*Figure 15.9*

**Note:    The values utilized on these examples are not necessarily the specification of a particular amplifier.  It is important to verify the specifications of the amplifier that will be utilized.**


This information is important when acquiring an amplifier.  Many times, we think that the capacity of the amplifier is defined by the brand or model of the amplifier.  For example, if we find an amplifier model XX2400, normally they tell us that it has a power of 2,400 watts, but they don't specify if this power is for each channel or if it is a bridge connection and how many ohms.

## Amperage consumption

It is important to take into consideration the consumption of the amplifier amperage in order to know the electrical connection that we are going to need and how much current the circuit is going to use. If we connect various amplifiers to the same circuit it is going to overload and it can cause the breaker from the electric panel to shut down.

<u>Serie connection of the speakers to the amplifier</u>

The speaker has a possivitve (+) and negative (-) terminals.

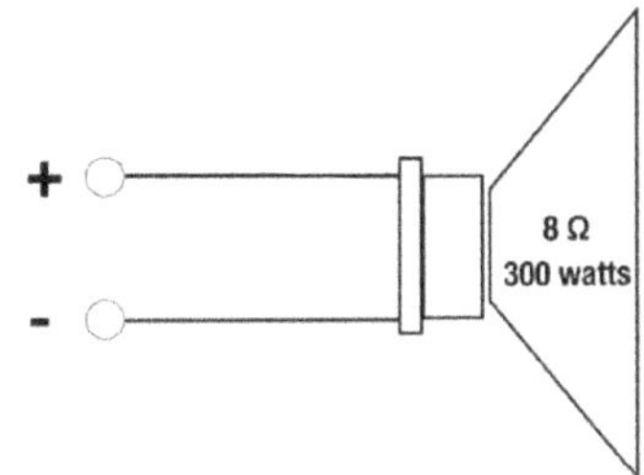



*Figure 15.10*

The Figure 15.11 show a speaker serie connection:

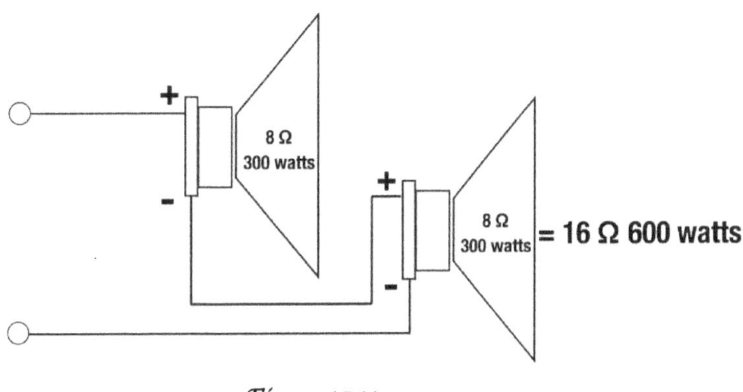



*Figure 15.11*

As you see in Figure 15.11, first, from the positive (+) terminal of the amplifier, connect one wire to the positive terminal of the speaker #1, then from the negative terminal of the speaker #1, connect a cable to the positive terminal of the speaker #2, and from the negative terminal of the second speaker, to the negative (-) terminal of the amplifier.

When you have a speaker serie connection, you have a sum of the speaker's ohms.  Two speakers of 8 Ω in serie sum a total of 16 Ω.  If each speaker are 300 watts, then the total will be 600 watts.

## Parallel connection of the speakers to the amplifier

The most common connection between the speakers and the amplifier is a parallel connection. As an example, we will use a speaker of 300 watts to 8 Ω.

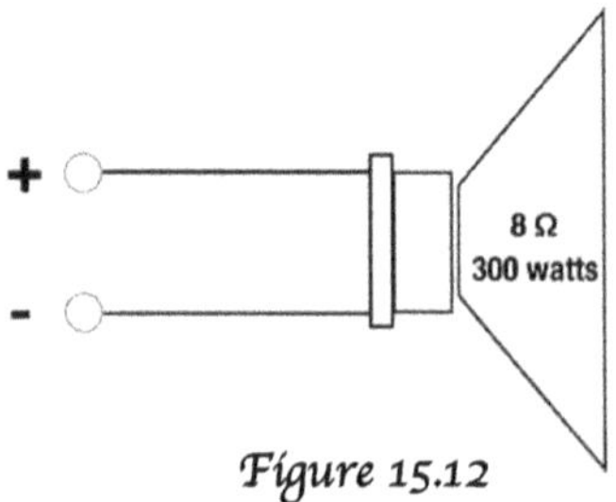


*Figure 15.12*

When we connect two 300-watt parallel speakers to 8 Ω, it is like having a 600-watt speaker at 4 Ω.

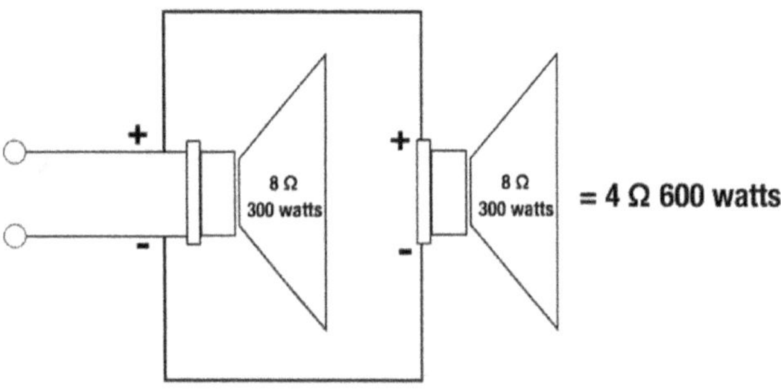


*Figure 15.13*

## Parallel connection of four speakers

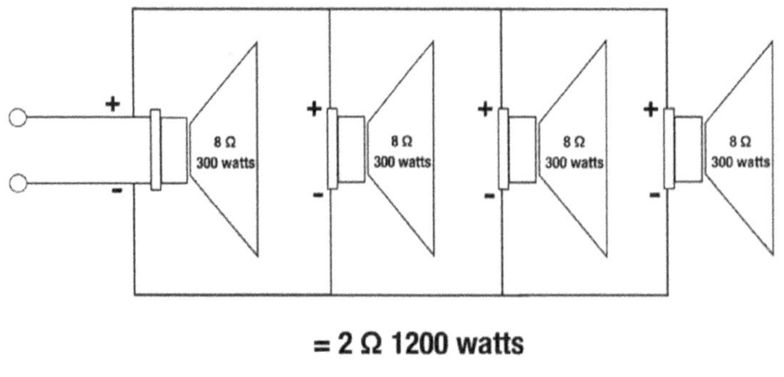


*Figure 15.14*

When we connect four parallel speakers from 300 watts to 8 Ω, it is like having a speaker from 1200 watts to 2 Ω.

<u>Recommendations</u>

1. The power of the amplifier must be greater than the RMS power of the speakers, to have amplification of reserve and to avoid distortion.
2. Note the descriptions of the amplifier (Figure 15.9). If the power capacity in watts to which it refers is:
    a. for each channel
    b. or if it refers to a bridge connection
    c. and how many ohms

# Chapter 16: The Mixer

In our audio system, the **console or mixer**, will be the equipment responsible for the *control and processing of different signals or audio sources*. These signals can come from microphones, musical instruments, instrument amplifier, audio player, computer and many more equipment.

Once the signal is received from the source to the mixer we can:

- increase the gain
- manage the frequency
- add effects
- group and mix
- sending the signal (to our main speakers, monitors, radio and television transmission, recorders, headphone, etc.)

Knowing this, the mixer:
- ***receives the signal (inputs)***
- ***process the signal***
- ***sends the signal (output)***

In the market we find different types of mixers, analog and digital. Next we will describe the basic functions of the analog mixer. This knowledge will help as a basis to manage the digital mixer as well.

## Basic parts of the mixer

In the box of the mixer we find:

- ✓ The Inputs (Figure 16.1)

    - o In the inputs we find terminals for the connectors:
        - XLR (connector utilized for the connection of balance signals)
        - ¼ Mono (connector utilized for the connection of unbalance signals)
        - ¼ Stereo **Insert** for connection of auxiliary equipment
        - RCA connector (two terminals, one for the right channel and the other for the left channel to receive audio signal)

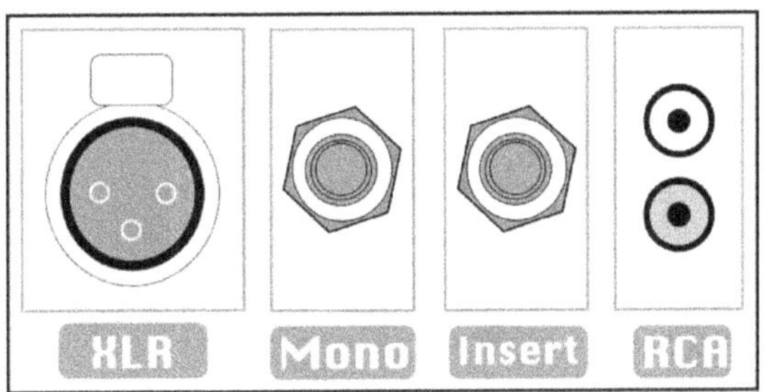

*Figure 16.1*

✓ Signal Processing Area (Figure 16.2)

- In each channel we will find:
  - **Gain**: it is used for pre-amplify the signal. This is identified in some mixers as TRIM.
  - **48v phantom power**:  small electrical power supply for condenser microphones.
  - **Low Cut**:  low cut frequency button
  - **Auxiliaries**: they send the signals through independent outputs to the "Master" outputs of the mixer. Regularly utilized to control the monitors, signal to recording or transmission, etc.
  - **Pre o Post** botton (See explanation on page 69)

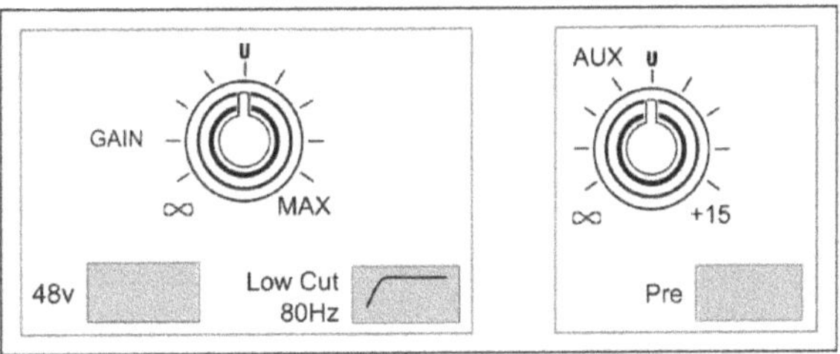



*Figure 16.2*

- **Ecualizer** (Figure 16.3)
  - High frequency knob
  - Mid frequency gain knob
  - Medium frequency selector
  - Low frequency pot

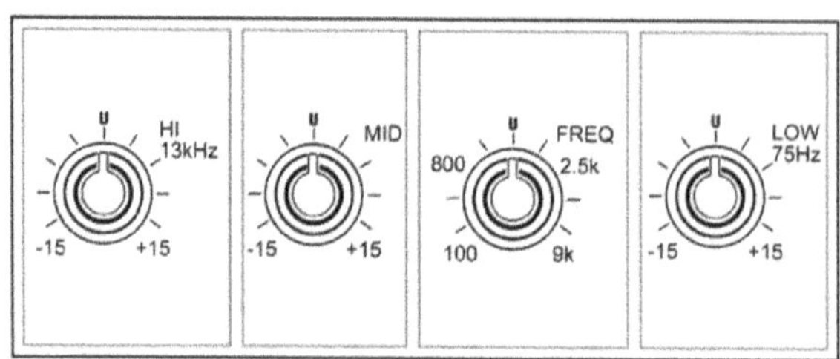

*Figure 16.3*

- **Effects** (Note: on some mixers)

- **Pan** (Figure 16.4):  with this button we can decide if we want the signal to be transmitted through the left channel, the right channel or both channels.
- **Mute Button:** channel off
- **Fader**
- **SOLO Button**:  this button help us see the input signal on the meters of the mixer, hear the signal in the headphone and know how much pre-amplification the signal needs.
- **Buttons to assig Sub Group 1-2 o L/R "left & right"**

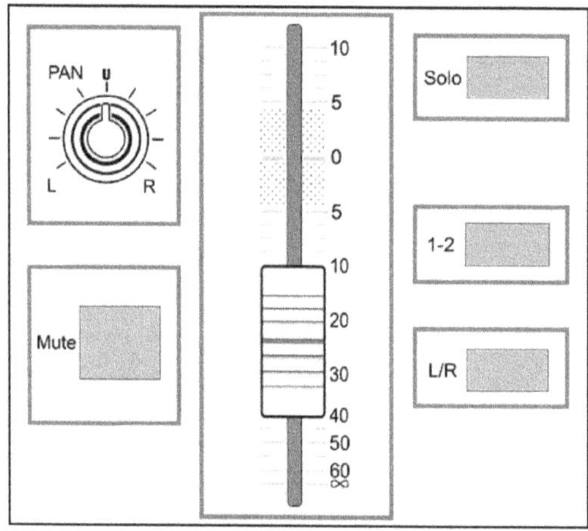

*Figure 16.4*

✓ Master volume section (Figure 16.5)

  o In this section we will find the Master volume controls of:
  - **Auxiliaries**
  - **Tape volume** (audio reproductor through the connection in the RCA input)
  - **Headphone volume**
  - **Headphone connection**

- **The Meters**
- **Sub Groups**
- **Master Volume Left and Right (Main)**

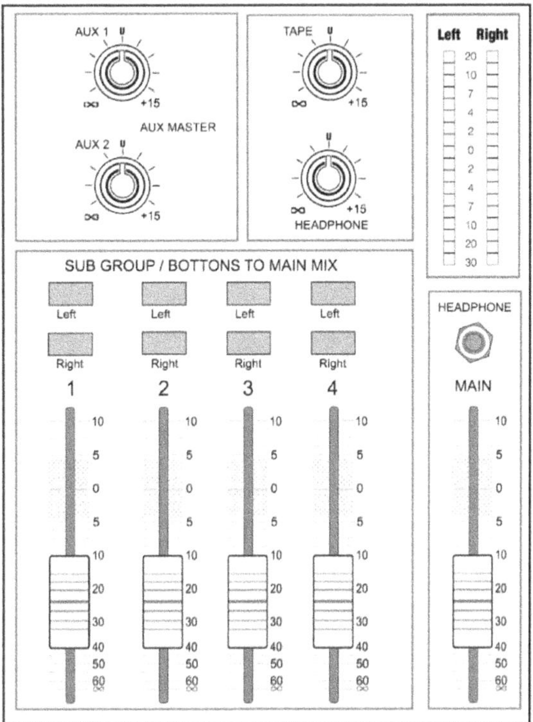

*Figure 16.5*

✓ Output Area (Figure 16.6)

    ○ The mixer will have output:

- **Master Output.** output to left channel, right channel and Mono
- **Sub Groups**
- **Auxiliaries**
- **RCA (for recording)**

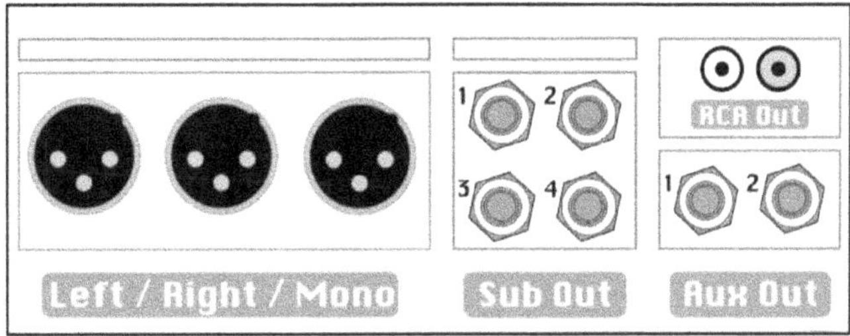


*Figure 16.6*

# The Mixer

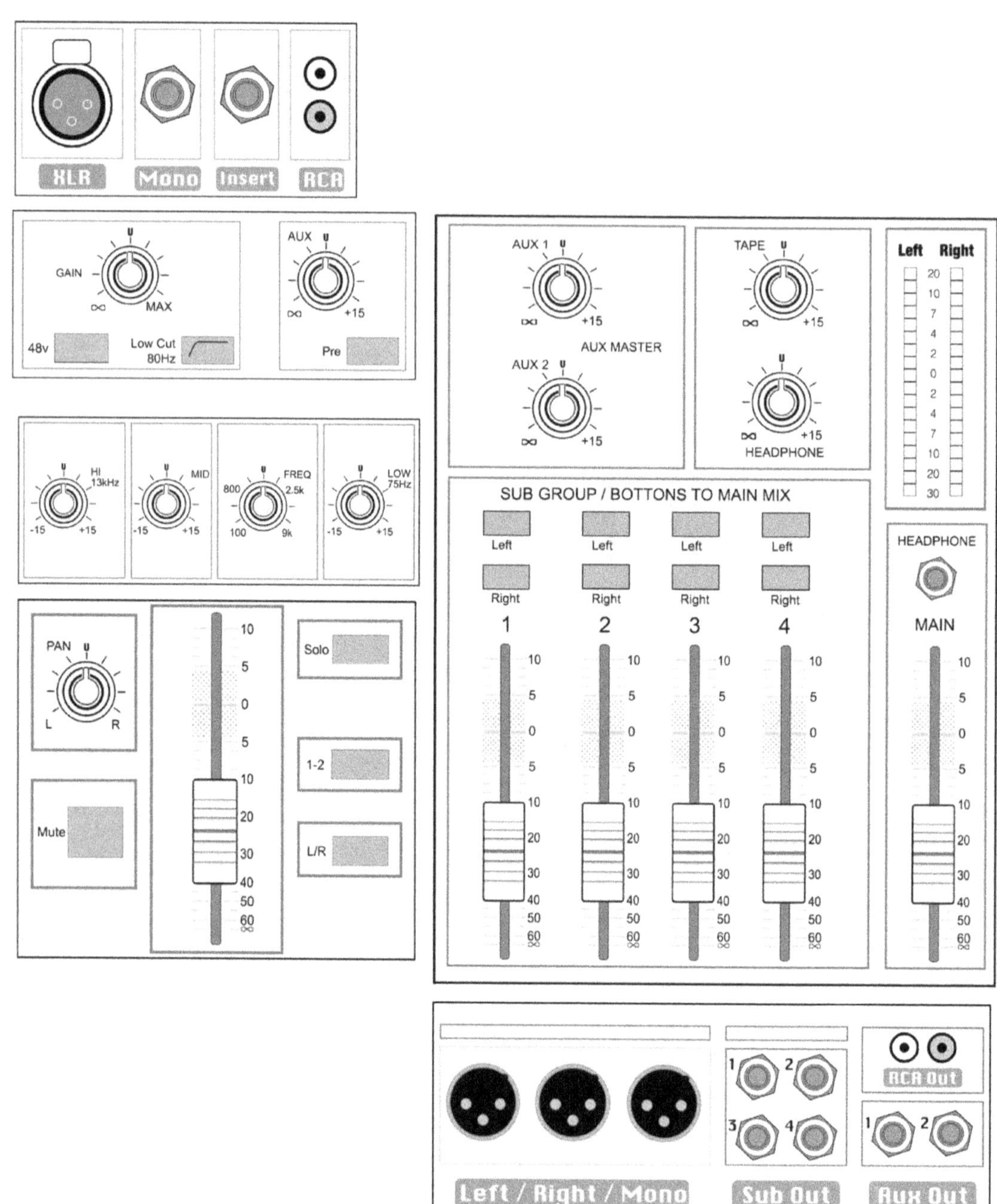



*Figure 16.7*

# Chapter 17: Basic Connections

Now that we know the parts of our audio system, we will provide some examples of equipment connections.

<u>Connection of 2 speakers and 2 subwoofers</u> (Figure 17.1)

Equipment needed for connection of main speakers and passive subwoofers:

- ✓ 1 Mixer
- ✓ 2 Speakers
- ✓ 2 Subwoofers
- ✓ 2 Amplifiers* (the capacity of the amplifiers will depend on the consumption of the speakers and subwoofers).
- ✓ 1 Crossover (for the subwoofer)
- ✓ Signal cables with XLR connectors
- ✓ Speaker cables with SpeakON or ¼ Mono connectors

1.  ***If we utilize speakers and active subwoofers, we do not need the amplifiers.***

Continuing with the following instructions, and using as a reference Figure 17.1, we will make the following connections:

1. From the Left output of the mixer, to the / Amp Ch1 input / From the Amp. Ch1 output, to the / "L" speaker input

2. From the "Right" output of the mixer, to the / Amp. Ch 2 input / From the Amp. Ch 2 output, to the / "R" speaker input

3. From the outputs "Left/Right" of the mixer, to the / Crossover Input / From the Crossover output, to the / Amp. Ch1 y Ch 2 Subwoofer input / From the Amp. Ch1 y Ch 2 output, to the / Subwoofer input "Sub L / Sub R"

Main Output
Left / Right / Mono
Main Speakers
Amplifier
Ch1
Ch2
Input
Output
Input
Output
L
R
Input
Crossover
Output
Subwoofer
Amplifier
Ch1
Ch2
Input
Output
Input
Output
Sub L
Sub R

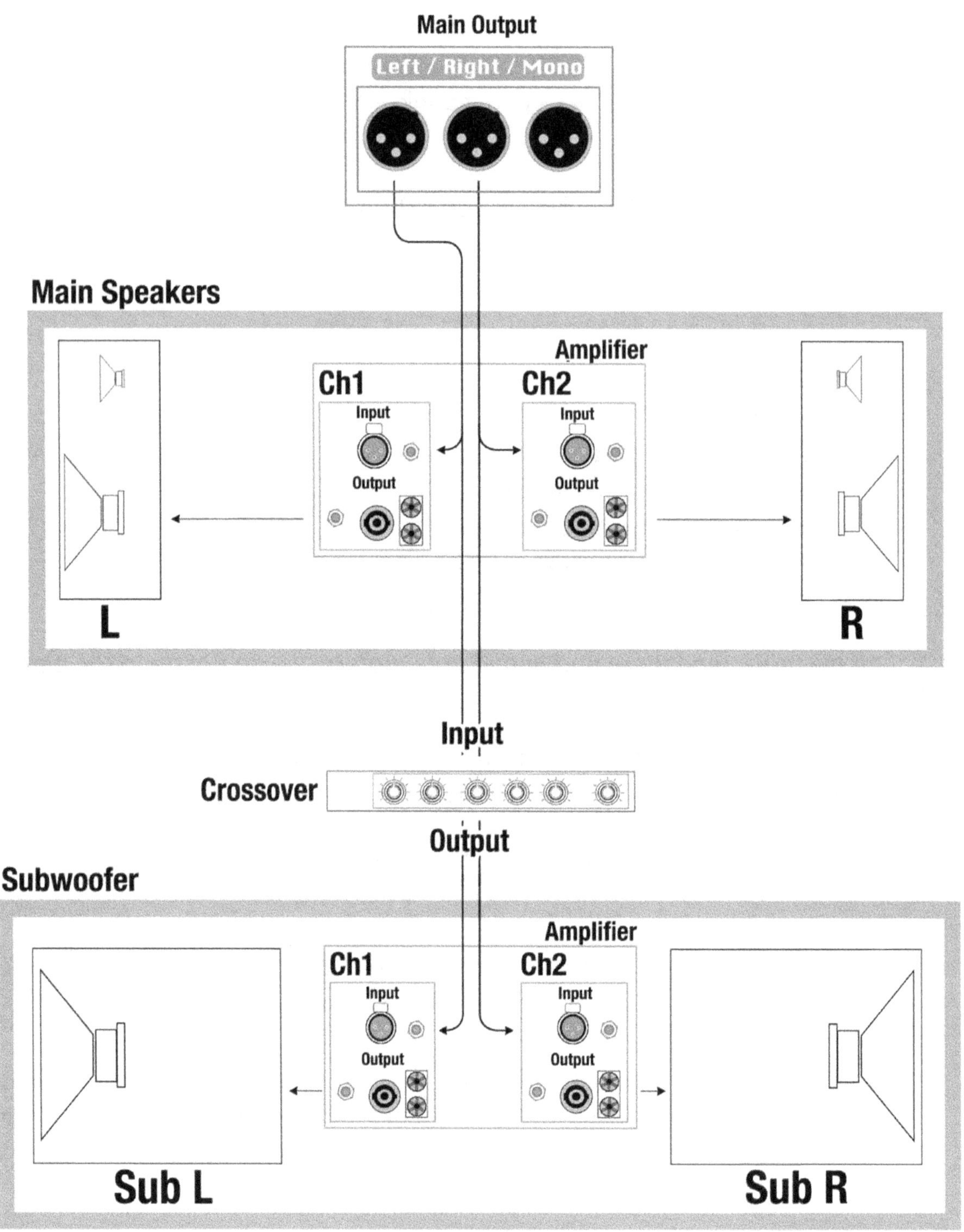

Figure 17.1

<u>Connection of 2 speakers and 2 monitors</u> (Figure 17.2)

Equipment needed in order to connect the main speakers and passive monitors:

- ✓ 1 Mixer
- ✓ 2 Speakers
- ✓ 2 Monitors
- ✓ 1 Equalizer*
- ✓ 2 Amplifiers**
- ✓ Signal cables with XLR connectors
- ✓ Speaker cables with SpeakON or ¼ Mono connectors

*** An equalizer should be installed in the output of the auxiliaries of the mixer in order to control the frequencies in the monitors.*

*** If we utilize speakers and active monitors, we do not need the amplifiers.*

<u>Instructions for connection</u>

1. From the Left output of the mixer, to the / Amp Input. Ch1 / From the Amp. Ch 1 output, to the / Speaker input "L"

2. From the Right output of the mixer, to the / Amp. Ch 2 / From the Amp. Ch 2 output, to the / Speaker input "R"

3. From the Aux 1 output of the mixer, to the / EQ Ch 1 input / From the EQ Ch 1 output, to the / Monitor Amp. Ch 1 input / From the Monitor Amp. Ch 1 output, to the / Monitor 1 input

4. From the Aux 2 output of the mixer, to the / EQ input Ch 2 / From the EQ Ch 2 output, to the / Monitor Amp. Ch 2 input / From the Monitor Amp. Ch 2 output, to the / Monitor 2 input

Main Output
Left / Right / Mono
Aux Out
Equalizer
Input
Output
EQ
Main Speakers
Amplifier
Ch1
Ch2
Input
Input
Output
Output
L
R
2 Monitor Mix
Amplifier
M1
Ch1
Ch2
M2
Input
Input
Output
Output

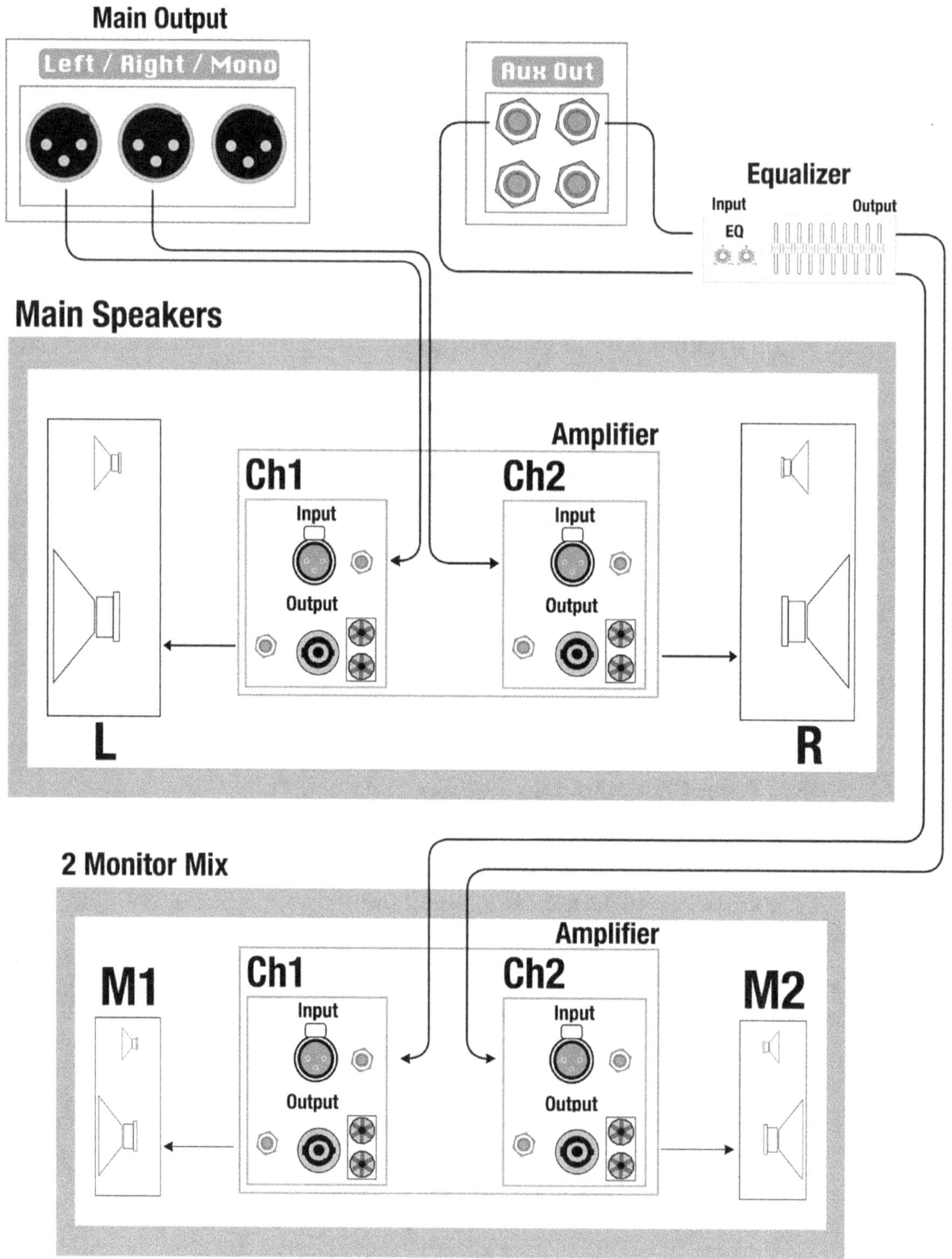

Figure 17.2

<u>Connection of 2 speakers, 2 subwoofers and 2 monitors</u> (Figure 17.3)

Equipment you will need for connecting main speakers and passive monitors:

- ✓  1 Mixer
- ✓  2 Speakers
- ✓  2 Monitors
- ✓  2 Subwoofers
- ✓  1 Equalizer
- ✓  1 Crossover
- ✓  3 Amplifiers
- ✓  Signal cables with XLR connectors
- ✓  Speakers cables with SpeakON or ¼ Mono connectors


<u>Instructions for connection</u>

1.  From the Left output of the mixer, to the / Amp. Ch 1 input / From the Amp. Ch 1 output, to the / Speaker input "L"

2.  From the Right console output, to the / Amp Input. Ch 2 / From the output Amp. Ch2, to the / Input Speaker "R"

3.  From the Left/Right console outputs, to the / Crossover Input / From the Crossover Output, to the / Amp Input. Ch1 and Ch 2 Sub / From the output Amp. Ch1 and Ch 2, to the Sub Input Sub Bass Sub L/Sub R

4.  From the Aux 1 console output, to the / EQ Input Ch1 / From the EQ Output Ch1, to the / Amp Input. Monitor Ch1 / From the output Amp. Monitor Ch1, to the / Input Monitor 1

5.  From the Aux 2 console output, to the / EQ Input Ch2 / From the EQ Output Ch2, to the / Amp Input. Monitor Ch2 / From the output Amp. Monitor Ch2, to the / Monitor 2 Input

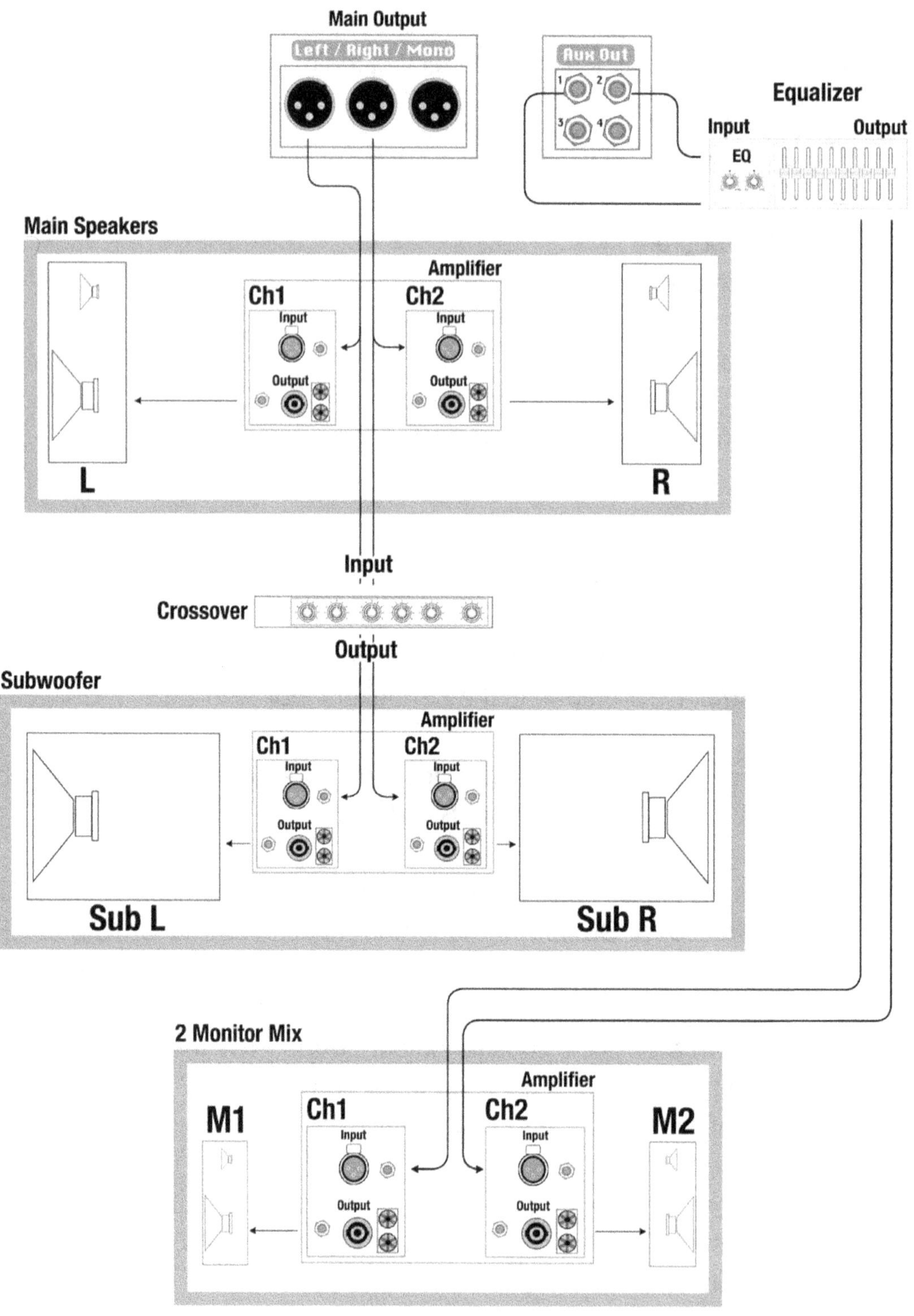


*Figure 17.3*

<u>Putting our equipment to work</u>

Let's verify that:
- ✓ The console output signal is connected to the amplifiers
- ✓ The speakers are connected to the amplifiers
- ✓ All the components of our equipment (EQ, "crossover", etc.) are on and the amplifiers have volume up

***Note: On active speakers the amplifier is inside the speaker and we have to check if it is on and if the volume on the speaker is up.***

<u>¿How to handle an audio signal?</u>

First step: A, B, C (Figure 17.4)

- ✓ The signal from a source (microphone, instrument, mp3, etc.) is received at the input of each channel of the console
- ✓ Press the Solo button to see the reflected signal strength in the Meters of the console.
- ✓ Turn the Gain button clockwise until the Metro lights go to zero "0". This will give us a reference of the input signal intensity.
- ✓ The green light that identifies the signal on the channel must be on.
- ✓ Check that the red "OL" signal overload light does not light up. An "OL" signal causes distortion in our audio system and can cause damage to our equipment, especially to the speakers.

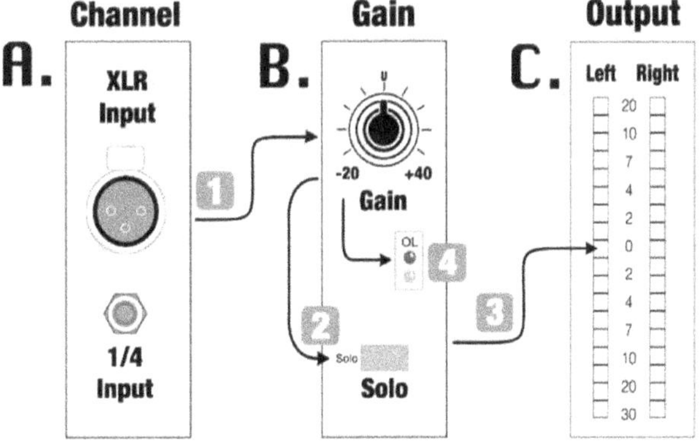


*Figure 17.4*

Second step: D, E (Figure 17.5)

1. Remove the Mute button
2. Assign the channel to Main. The assignment can be to Main or Sub Groups. If we choose the Sub Groups we must keep in mind that the Sub Groups must be assigned to the Main to output the audio through the main speakers.
3. Move the Fader from Main to zero "0"
4. We raise the "fader" of channel volume, little by little

***With this we should listen to the audio in our speakers.***

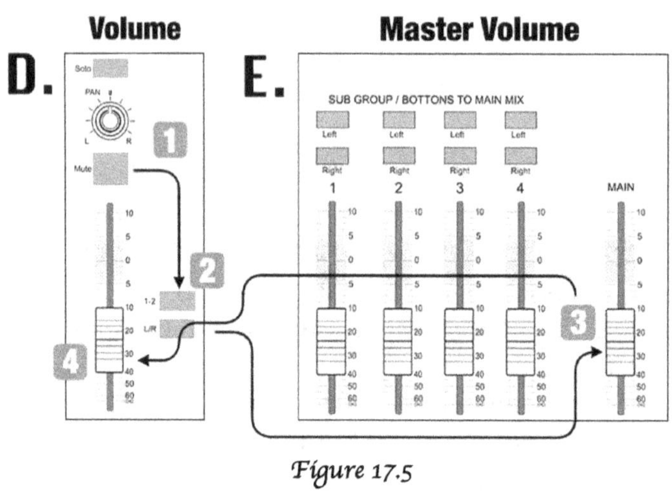


*Figure 17.5*

Third step: F, G, H (Figure 17.6)

1. Add equalization to the signal
2. We send the signal to the monitors through the buttons of the Ausiliaries.
   ✓ Pre/Post button: If this button ***is not pressed*** "Post", the channel signal goes through channel equalization and the auxiliary volume will be affected by the main channel volume controlled by the fader

✓ If we have this "Pre" button ***pressed***, the channel signal go directly to the auxiliary output without having passed the equalization of the channel and without any alteration by the main volume of the channel controlled by the fader.

3. Using the "PAN" button, we can handle the signal by sending it only to the left channel, the right channel or in the middle position to both channels.
4. The Low Cut button is used for signals that do not require low frequencies such as voice.
5. Press the 48v button when a condenser microphone is connected to the channel.

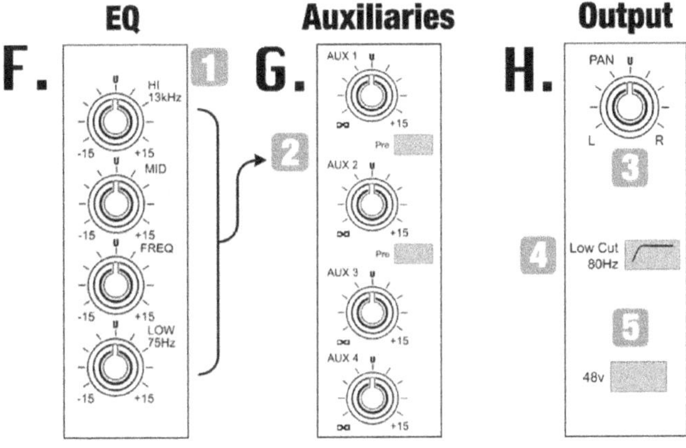


*Figure 17.6*

# Chapter 18:  Microphones

The microphone is the first component in the audio system chain.  With it we can capture a signal provenient of sound source such as voice, musical instruments, instrument amplifiers, etc. It is a **transducer**, capable of converting an acoustic signal into an electrical signal. Once converted to an electrical signal, it can be manipulated with the audio system. There are two (2) types of microphones very common: the dynamic and the condenser.

## Dynamic Microphones

**Dynamic microphones** are robust, resistant to moisture, and a high level of gain can be obtained before feedback occurs. We will describe its operation below.

A coil surrounds a magnet that forms a magnetic field. The coil is suspended so that it can have movement. A membrane or diaphragm vibrates when it receives the sound wave and that vibration causes movement in the coil. The movement of the coil generates an electrical voltage at its terminals, thus converting the acoustic signal into an electrical signal.

Dynamic microphones **do not need power supply** to operate.

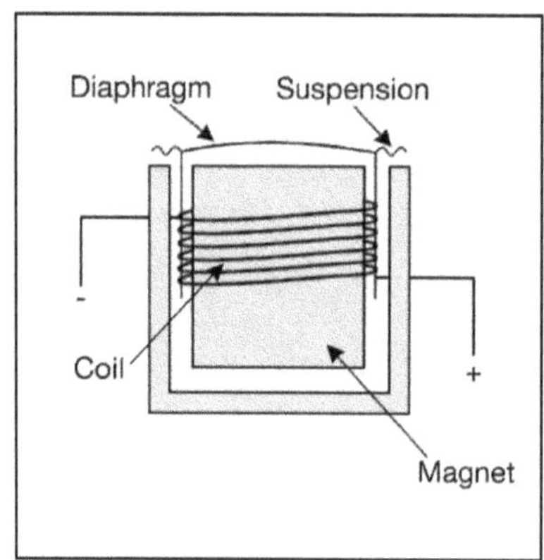


*Figure 18.1*
*Capsule of dynamic microphone*

# Condenser Microphones

The **condenser microphones** unlike the dynamic ones, generates the electrical signal by means of an electric field instead of a magnetic field. They have a high-quality output, they are more accurate, and have a high response to frequency. They can be more sensitive to feedbacks. We will describe its operation below.

Its construction is based on a diaphragm made of metal, or plastic coated metal, and a back plate. An electric charge is applied that creates an electric field between the diaphragm and the plate. When the sound wave causes the diaphragm to vibrate, the variation of the space between the diaphragm and the plate is what produces the electrical signal.

The condenser microphones **need a power supply for its operation**, known as a phantom power. The amount of voltage applied to the microphone by means of the "phantom power" is 48v.

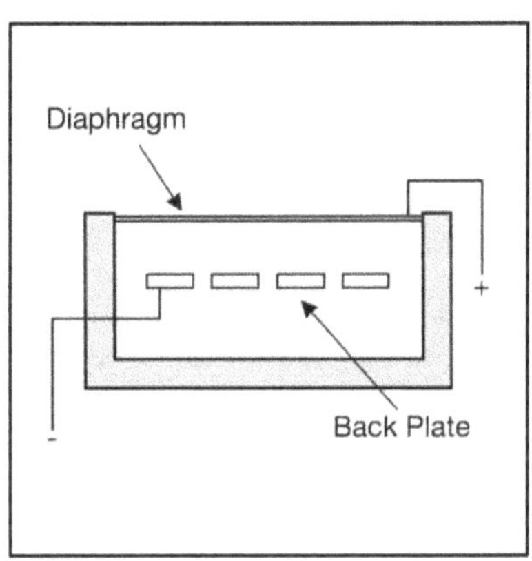


*Figure 18.2*
*Condenser microphone capsule*

# Characteristics of the Microphones

Knowing how the microphone picks up the acoustic signal and converts it into an electrical signal, there are several very important characteristics that we should consider:

1. the polar pattern
2. its response to the frequency
3. the proximity effect

# Directionality of the Microphones

As we already know, with the microphone we want to capture the signal coming from a source; the voice, an instrument, an instrument amplifier, the environment, etc. To describe the pickup characteristic of the microphone, a graph known as the *polar pattern* is used.

Within the different categories, the microphone with the *omnidirectional* polar pattern captures the signal coming from all directions. In the other polar patterns, it is sought that it has a point of greater capture of the signal, but while it has points of rejection of the unwanted signals.

The different polar patterns are known as:
1. Omnidirectional
2. Cardioid
3. Super-cardioid
4. Hyper-cardioid
5. Bi-directional

# Polar Patterns

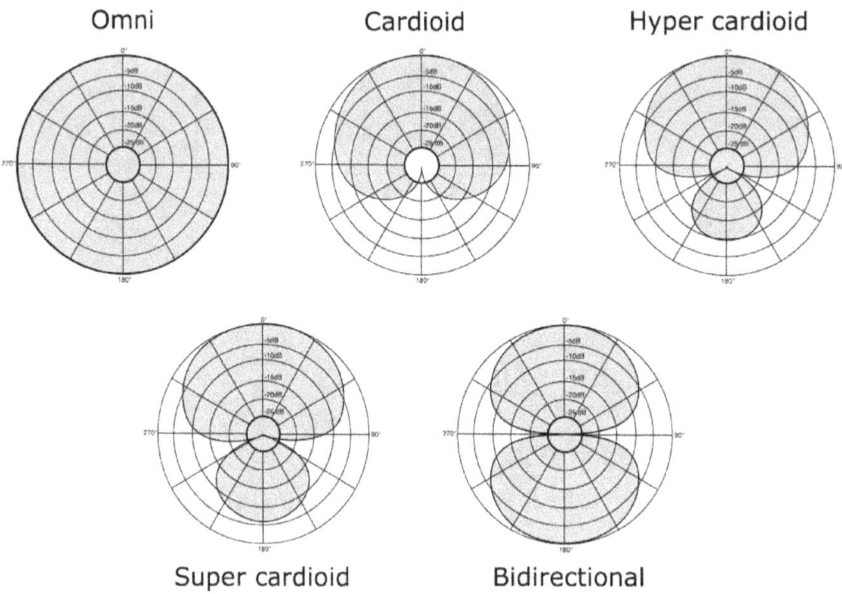


*Figure 18.3*
*Different polar patterns*

The following graphs explain the polar pattern of a cardioid microphone:

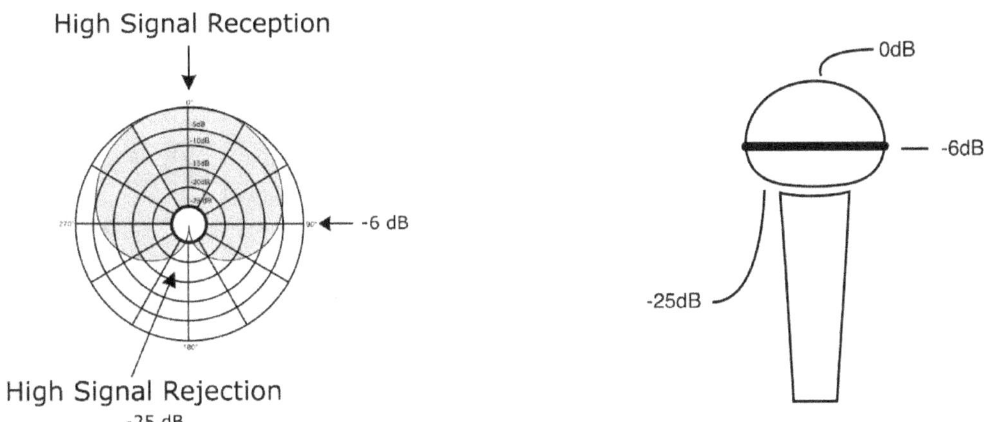


*Figure 18.4*
*Cardioid polar pattern*

Table of comparison of the different polar patterns of microphones

| Description | Omni Directional | Cardioid | Hyper Cardioid | Super Cardioid | Bidirectional |
|---|---|---|---|---|---|
| Coverage | 360° | 131° | 115° | 105° | 90° |
| Maximum rejection | ---- | 180° | 126° | 110° | 90° (on the sides) |
| Rear rejection in dB (relative to the front) | 0 | 25 dB | 12 dB | 6 dB | 0 |

## Response to the Microphone Frequency

The frequency response curve is one of the most valuable tools that allows to predict how the microphone will sound. A microphone with a flat response is one that could reproduce all frequencies at the same level, 0 dB. It is equally sensitive to all frequencies. By means of a graph we can know the design of the microphone and its behavior in the different frequencies.

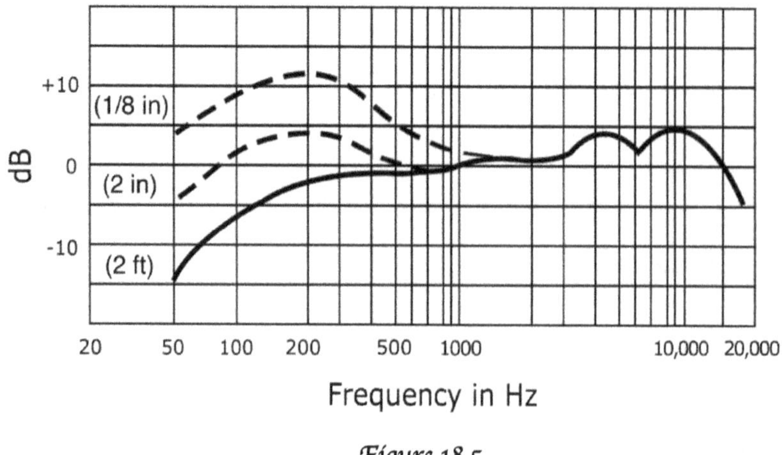


*Figure 18.5*

In the graph of Figure 18.5 we can find the following information:

1. The solid black line tells us what the microphone response is at two (2) feet.

2. At two (2) inches we will have an increase in low frequencies, where the highest point of the graph reaches + 4dB.

3. When approaching 1/8 of an inch to the microphone we will obtain an increase of about + 11db at its highest point.

*Figure 18.6*
*Proximity of the microphone a distance of 1/8 of an inch*

# Proximity Effect

The proximity effect is another characteristic of microphones and is related to the increase of low frequencies in relation to high frequencies. This happens when the distance between the microphone and the source that produces the signal is cut off. It is recommended to use a high pass filter to control the excess of low frequencies.

*Figure 18.7*

# The Microphones and the Sound Check

The sound check is the moment when the sound engineer is ready to listen to the instruments, the singers, the pre-recorded sequences and everything related to the presentation of the event. It is in this sound test that the levels of the signals, the equalization, the processors, the monitors, effects, etc. are adjusted of each of the signals that are received in the console.

It is very important that both the musical instruments and the singers send a good signal with which the sound engineer can work. For example, when the guitarist is asked to play the guitar, the guitarist raises the volume of the guitar so that the sound engineer can have a clear reference to the sound of the guitar.

With the singers, it is the same. When they are asked to use the microphone so that the sound engineer receives the signal from the voice, what is sought is for the microphone to obtain a good sound reference for the voice, a good volume. The job of the microphone is to receive the acoustic signal and change it to an electrical signal. What you receive, is what you are going to process.

## Strong Signal, Weak Signal

Now, the singer is the one who produces the signal with the voice, but at the same time he needs to hear a reference of his voice on the monitors. If the sound produced by the voice is low volume, this will be a difficulty for the sound engineer.

When the microphone signal enters the console, the first adjustment that the soundman makes is to pre-amplify the signal. This will give him an optimum level to be able to process it. If the voice is strong, he will not need to raise the gain much on the console and therefore prevent unwanted noise from being captured by the microphone. This will also allow the sound engineer to send a good voice reference to the singer on the monitors.

If the voice is weak, the sound engineer will have to raise the level of preamp a lot to get a good volume of the voice, but at the same time unwanted noise will be captured by the microphone and the possibility of feedback between the monitors and the microphone. Not getting a strong signal from the voice may be due to the following reasons:

1. The singer speaks very low, without strength or with fear.
    a. If the acoustic sound received by the microphone is weak, the electrical signal will be weak.
2. The singer is very far from the microphone.
    a. It is not the same that the singer is at 1/8 inch away from the microphone than at 1 feet away.

## Microphone Sensitivity

This characteristic refers to how sensitive the microphone is when the sound wave reaches the capsule. Depending on its design and construction, you will need volume adjustment in the console gain to obtain a line signal.

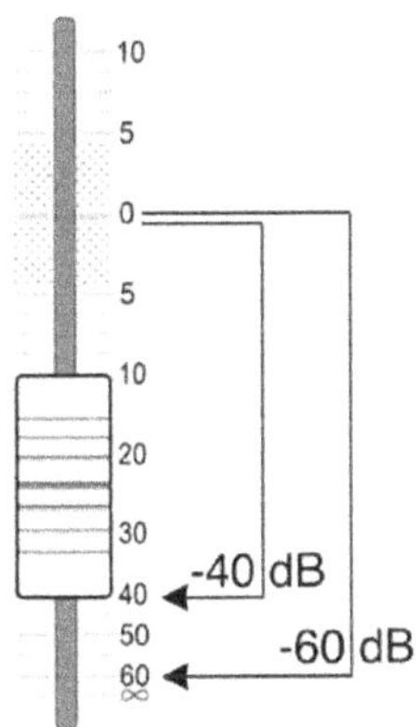


*Figure 18.8*

In the graph, the value of 0 dB represents the optimum volume of operation. A microphone with a sensitivity of -60 dB will need more volume than one with a sensitivity of -40 dB. The closer it is to 0 dB, the better.

## Use of the Microphone and Recommendations

- The correct way to grip the microphone is to leave the cover of the capsule uncovered, so that a polar pattern change does not occur.

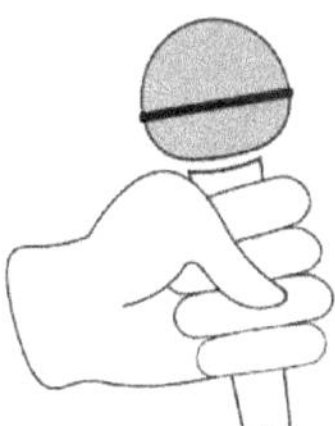

*Figure 18.9*

- Covering the capsule of a microphone with a cardioid polar pattern by hand will cause the microphone to become omnidirectional.

- It will also cause a change in the microphone equalization.

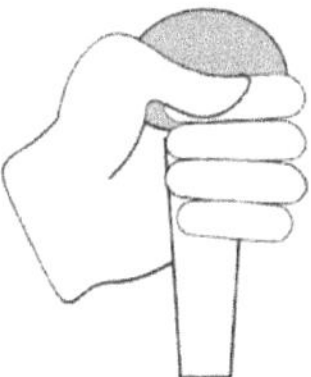

*Figure 18.10*

- Pointing the microphone direct to the monitor is one of the causes of feedback production on the monitors and in the system.

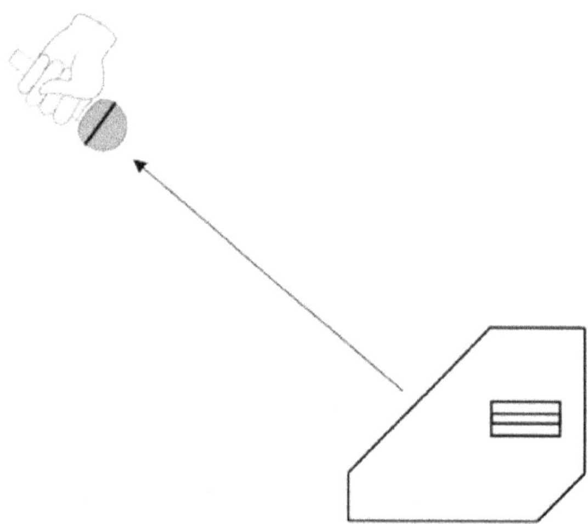

*Figure 18.11*

# Chapter 19:  Signal Processing

One of the main challenges of the technician or sound engineer is to ensure that the audio system reproduces in a natural, clear and balanced way the sound processed and reproduced by the audio system. Several factors will play an important role: the acoustics of the premises, the size of the room or if the activity is outside, the sound equipment that will be used, etc., but the way we listen to the sound will be the most important.

In our equipment, the speakers will be responsible for converting the electrical signal into an acoustic signal. There are many speakers of different:

- Sizes
- Designs
- Applications
- Coverage
- Power
- Materials
- Electronic

With the design, it is sought to obtain in the speakers that have a ***flat frequency response***. What does this mean? This means that the low, medium and high frequencies are perceived as being at the same level, with the same amplitude (Figure 19.1).

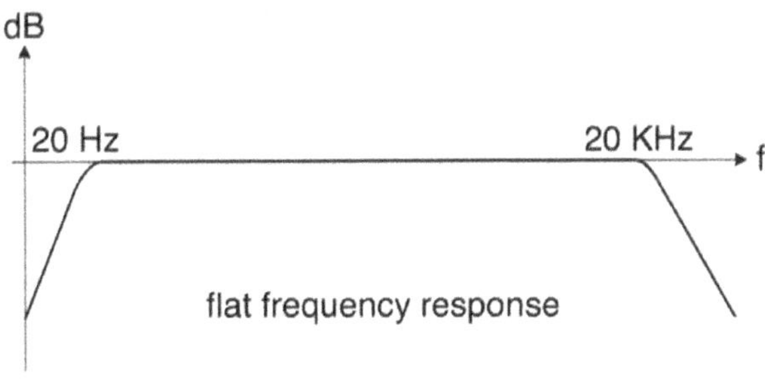


Figure 19.1

Any alteration or exaggerated amplitude of any frequency range will cause discomfort in the auditory perception and damage to our equipment. It is not the same to feel the marked presence of the sub bass in some musical genre, which then disproportionately increases the frequencies of the sub bass causing distortion in the speakers, "feedbacks" at low frequencies and an imbalance in the musical program. That the bass and the drums are heard in such a way that the sounds generated by the other instruments and members of the band are not clearly perceived, indicates that something is wrong.

When we see a graph of a sound obtained in a spectrum analyzer, having a flat response does not mean that all frequencies will be seen on the graph at the same sound pressure level (Figure 19.2). There will always be a wave movement of the frequencies, because the sound is the result of the movement of air in the form of a wave.

Let's use this example: When we are facing a body of water like the sea and we say, "the sea is like a plate", we mean that it looks as if it is still, but in reality, it has movement. Large waves are not seen, but there is undulation in the water.

The same happens with sound. To refer to the system having a flat response, is that there is no drastic alteration in any of these registers (Figure 19.2).

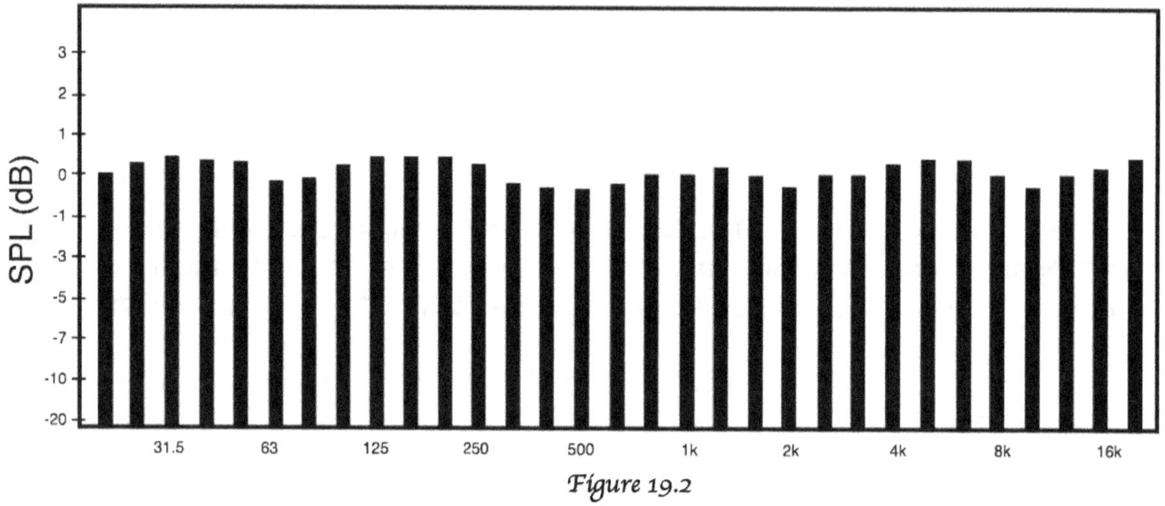


*Figure 19.2*

Seeing a frequency response as in the graph of Figure 19.2, is considered a flat response of the sound obtained in a real-time spectrum analyzer.

One of the first things we must do is to balance our sound system. For this a graphic equalizer is used in the output of the console and spectrum analyzer RTA (we will discuss the topic of the RTA below). Let's see the characteristics of the graphic equalizer.

# Graphic Equalizer

The graphic equalizer is one of the signals processing equipment that we use in our sound equipment. Normally applied to the main outputs of the console are auxiliary outputs for monitors, sub groups or for some instrument.

The graphic equalizers are divided into bands of certain specific frequencies and have several fixed bands, usually between 5 to 31 bands. In audio systems, graphic equalizers of 15 bands, 2/3 octaves or 31 bands, 1/3 octave, and come with 1 and 2 channels are regularly used. Each band will be assigned a certain specific frequency. Figure 19.3 presents a 31-band equalizer and 1 single channel.

Frontal Panel

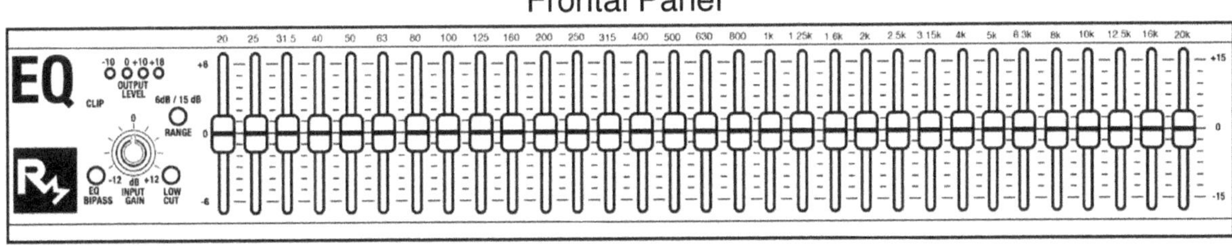

*Figure 19.3*

On the back panel of the single-channel equalizer, we will find an input with XLR, a Mono ¼ connection and an output with XLR and Mono ¼ connections. If the equalizer is two (2) channels, it will have two (2) inputs and two (2) outputs (Figure 19.4).

Posterior Panel

*Figure 19.4*

In the following table (Figure 19.5), we will find the standard frequencies that are used for the 2/3 octave band (15 band) and 1/3 octave band (31 band) equalizers. The frequency of 20Hz is the most severe and the frequency of 20kHz is the sharpest.

| f (Hz) | 2/3 | 1/3 | f (Hz) | 2/3 | 1/3 |
|---|---|---|---|---|---|
| 20 | | x | 800 | | x |
| 25 | x | x | 1,000 | x | x |
| 31.5 | | x | 1,250 | | x |
| 40 | x | x | 1,600 | x | x |
| 50 | | x | 2,000 | | x |
| 63 | x | x | 2,500 | x | x |
| 80 | | x | 3,150 | | x |
| 100 | x | x | 4,000 | x | x |
| 125 | | x | 5,000 | | x |
| 160 | x | x | 6,300 | x | x |
| 200 | | x | 8,000 | | x |
| 250 | x | x | 10,000 | x | x |
| 315 | | x | 12,500 | | x |
| 400 | x | x | 16,000 | x | x |
| 500 | | x | 20,000 | | x |
| 630 | x | x | | | |

*Figure 19.5*

When all the keys are in their central position, there is no alteration in frequencies (Figure 19.3). If one of the keys is moved to a value of +12 dB, the center point of that band will be emphasized at the frequency represented by the band, but nearby frequencies will also be affected by the adjustment made to a smaller amount. Example: the key from 63Hz to 12 dB (Figure 19.6 and 19.7).

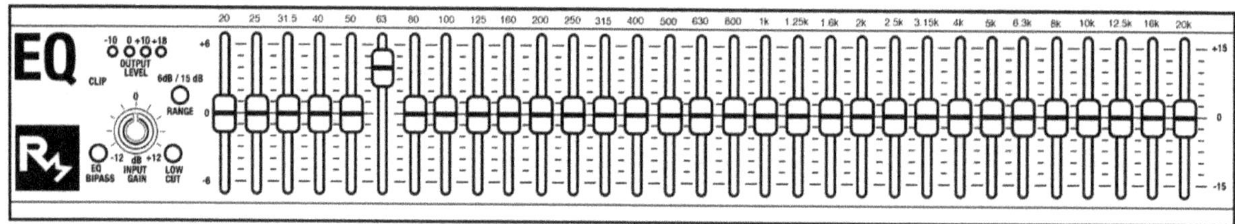


*Figure 19.6*

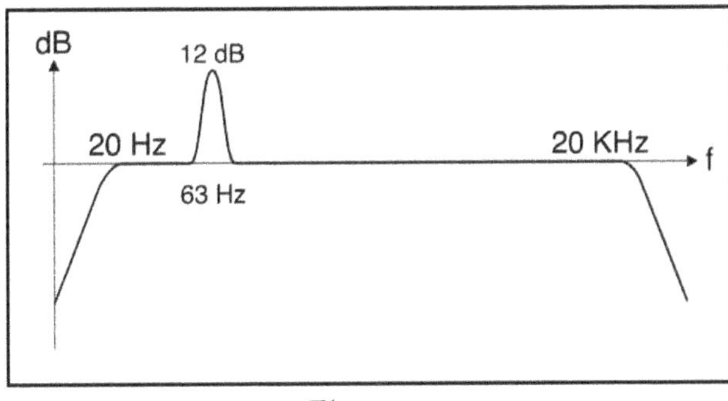



*Figure 19.7*

If we attenuate the key of the frequency from 1 KHz to -12 dB, the frequency response will be as follows (Figure 19.8 and 19.9):

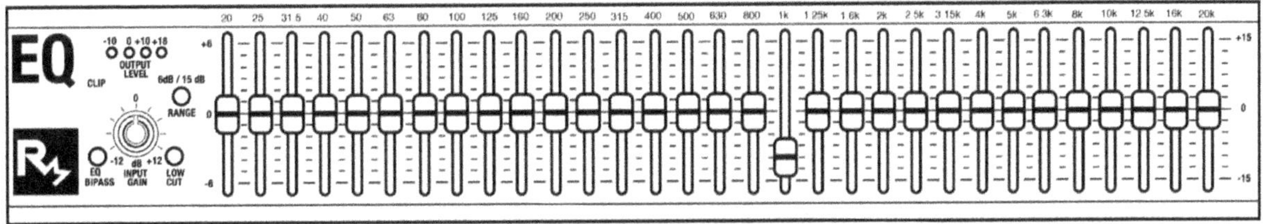

*Figure 19.8*

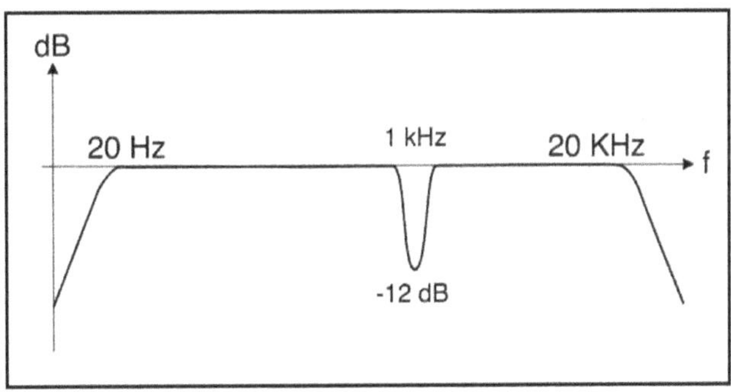



*Figure 19.9*

When we make several band adjustments in the equalizer, we will have as a result the following frequency response (Figure 19.10 and 19.11):

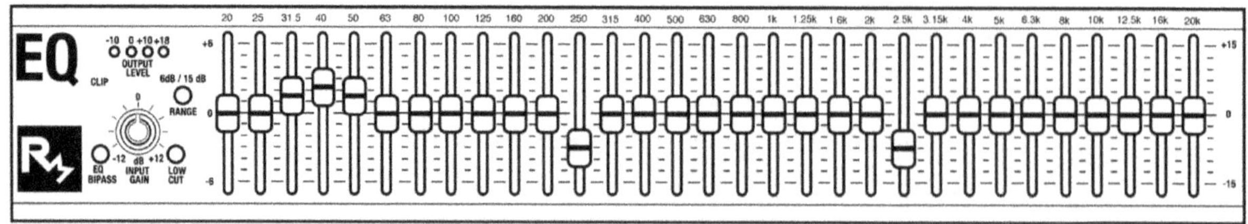

Figure 19.10

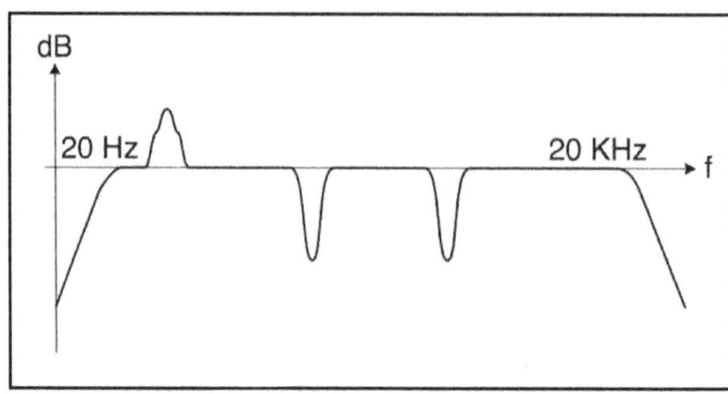


Figure 19.11

These examples provide us with important knowledge, since the adjustments made to the equalizer will have a direct effect on the frequencies and, therefore, on the resulting sound.

Graphic EQs are normally used:

1. In the main output of the console, with the purpose of equalizing the resulting sound of the main speakers of our audio system, together with the acoustic environment.

2. In each auxiliary output destined to the mix of monitors, it looks for the control of the frequencies in each of the mixtures.

The connection of the equalizer in each output is for having a **general adjustment of each mix**, and not to be used in the individual equalization of microphones and instruments. For the individual equalization of the instruments, the **parametric equalizer** (that each channel has in the console), will be used.

The graph in Figure 19.12 shows a connection of the equalizers in the main outputs of the console, known as the main mix, and in the auxiliary outputs, known as the mix of monitors. In digital consoles the graphic equalizers are integrated into the console, and assigned to the corresponding output.

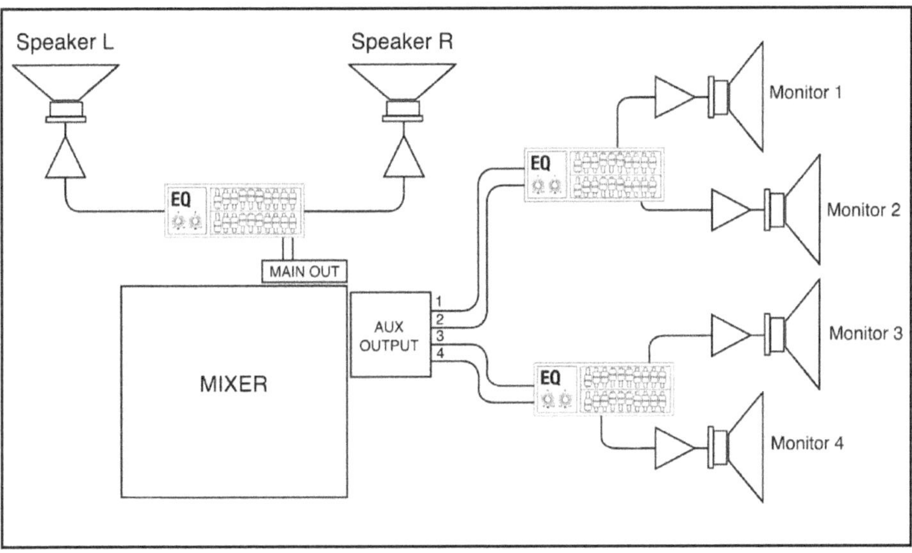



*Figure 19.12*

## Inserts

The console has a connection called "insert". This will be found in each channel and in the main output "Main Out" of the console. This connection is used to send the signal to an external device such as an equalizer, compressor, effect, etc. The equipment receives the signal, processes it and then sends it back to the console.

For this connection, you will need a cable with a stereo connector on one end of the cable and two mono connectors on the other end (Figure 19.13).

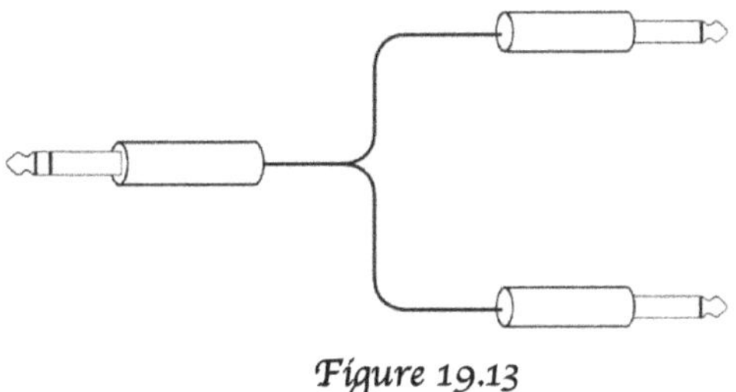

*Figure 19.13*

The stereo connector has the function of sending and receiving the signal in the console through the "insert" connection, at the other end the signal is sent by one of the mono connectors, it enters the equipment, and it exit the equipment through the other mono connector.

<u>Equalizer Connection in the "Insert" of the Console Output</u>

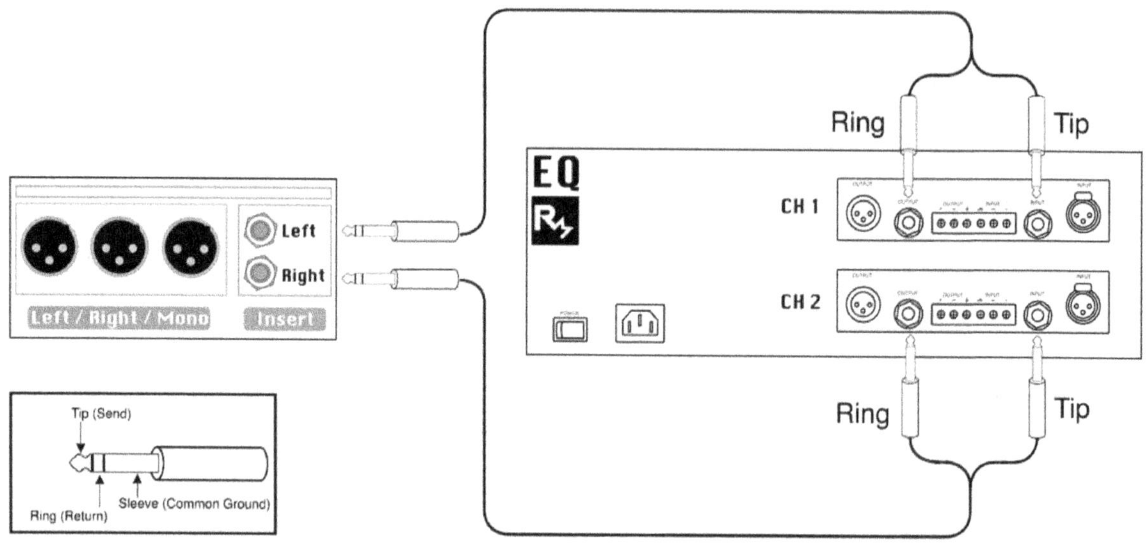



*Figure 19.14*

## <u>Parametric Equalizer</u>

Unlike the graphic equalizer, which has a specific frequency assigned to each band, in the parametric equalizer you can choose several parameters and the adjustments are made by means of potentiometers used to increase or decrease the desired function.

Figure 19.15 – Types of adjustments you can make are:
1. Choose the frequency
2. The amplitude (boost / cut)
3. The width of the band (bandwidth), identified with the letter Q

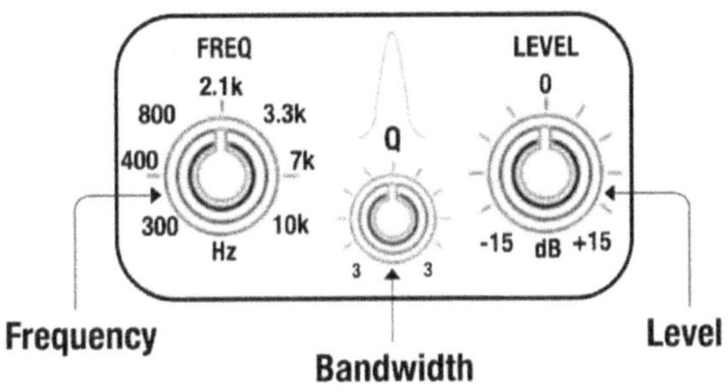


*Figure 19.15*

The process for adjusting the equalizer is:

1. Choose the frequency that you want to adjust.
2. Determine if we are going to increase or decrease the frequency.
3. Determine the width of the band (Q). The wider the band, the more frequencies close to the chosen frequency will be affected. In the graph of Figure 19.16 we can see different types of bandwidth.

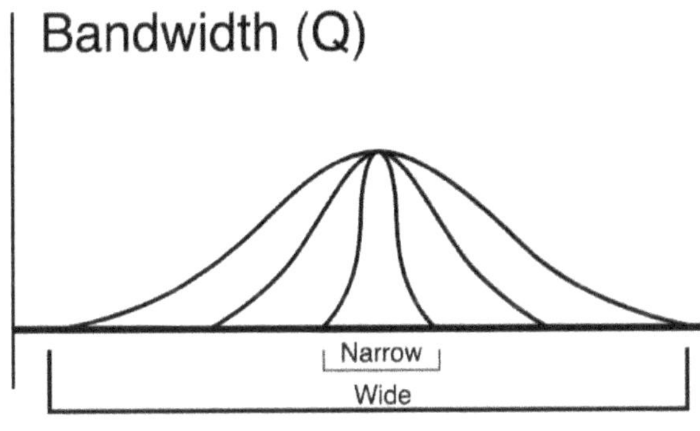


*Figure 19.16*

This equalizer is a powerful tool in the management of tone control in sound. For example, we can get:

- Alter the original sound of the signal.
- Strengthen the presence of the drum or bass drum.
- Eliminate frequencies that are not in the instrument or voice record.
- Add color or tonality to the signal. This is linked to the individual sound that identifies the instrument.

<u>Front Panel of the Parametric Equalizer</u>

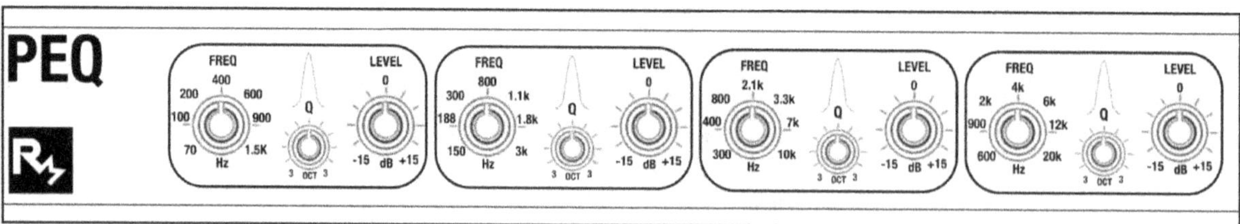


If the parametric EQ is four bands, we will find an adjustment for:

- the lows
- the medium-lows
- the medium-highs
- the highs


<u>Differences Between the Graphic Equalizer and the Parametric Equalizer</u>

| Graphic EQ | Parametric EQ |
|---|---|
| The frequencies are assigned to each band. | We can choose the frequency that we want to alter. |
| The bandwidth is established. | We can alter the width of the band (Q). |

# Chapter 20:  Dynamic Processors

A good final mix will be the one that produces a balanced volume as a result. There are signals that are received in the console with multiple volume variations. In the musical program, a singer, for example, will sing sections with little intensity and at other times of great intensity. This will cause a volume change in the signal.

When we are making a live sound, where we have multiple musical instruments and multiple microphones, the use of equipment that processes the signal helps achieve a better result in the final mix.

Many times, we need:

1.  Control the volume of the voice, of an instrument or of the mix in general.
2.  That a microphone closes or opens so that it does not pick up sound at any specific time.
3.  Improve the result in the final mix.

We can achieve this with the equipment that we will see next.


## The Compressor

The compressor is used to control the amplitude of a signal.

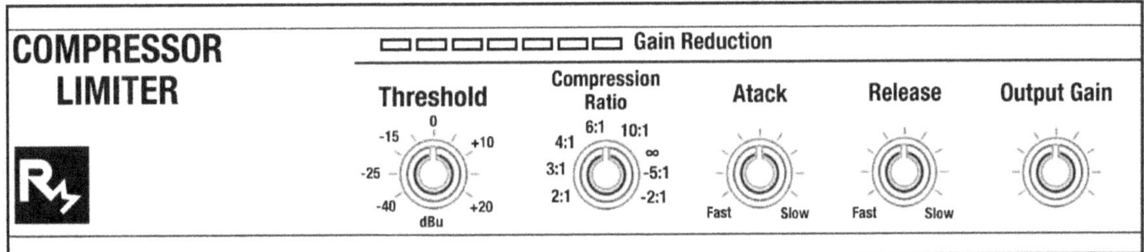


*Figure 20.1*


How does it work? The first thing we must determine is the level of volume that we want, whether it is an instrument, the voice or the mix.

Normally, we want the signal to be kept in the meter of the console in a specific range. For example, if we look at the meter of the console, locate the point where it marks the 0 dB (Figure 20.2).

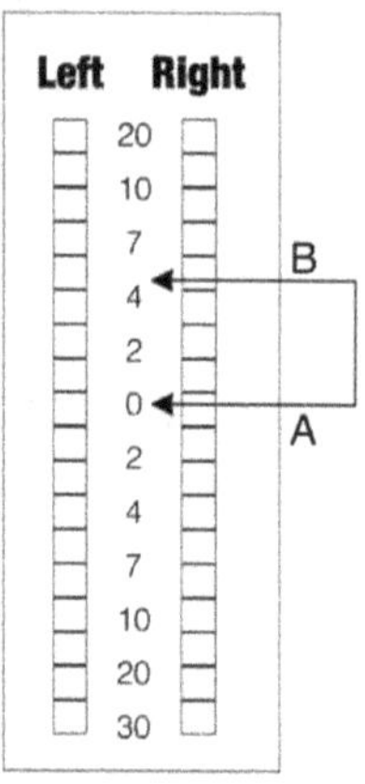


*Figure 20.2*

So, if we want the signal to be maintained between point A to point B (Figure 20.2), this is between 0 dB and +5 dB, we should make the adjustments in the compressor to get the signal to stay in this parameter and do not exceed +5 dB.

When the signal reaches the desired volume, if there is an excess volume of the signal, the compressor will help to attenuate it according to the settings that we have assigned. The adjustments made to the compressor are:

1.  Threshold

2.  Rate

3.  Attack

4.  Release

## Threshold

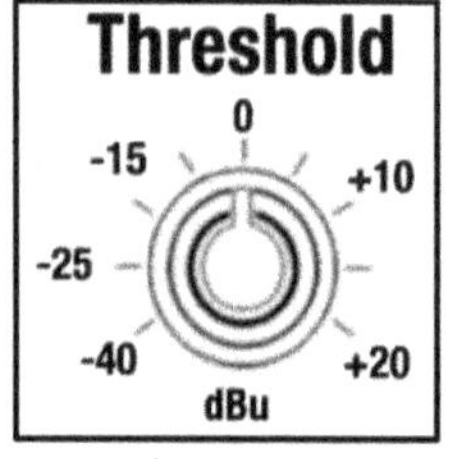


*Figure 20.3*

The threshold is the point where we want the compressor to start processing the signal. Let's say that the signal has a good gain when it reaches 0 dB in the meter of the console, and that after that point we want any excess volume of the signal to be controlled. With the threshold, we will achieve this adjustment (Figure 20.3).

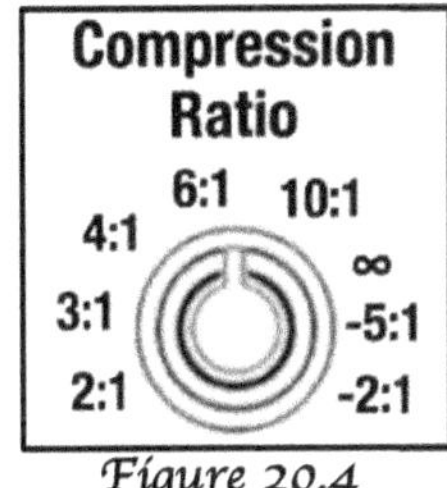



*Figure 20.4*

The second adjustment is the one that will indicate how many dB will be reduced from the signal after the point that we have determined. For this, a ratio scale between two values is used (Figure 20.4).

We will find a potentiometer containing the following scale, 2: 1, 3: 1, 4: 1, 6: 1, 8: 1.

On the scale, 1: 1 means there is no compression. Let's see a compression setting of 3: 1. The first number indicates the amount of compression in decibels and the second number tells us that 1 dB will be generated for each compression made. When the signal exceeds the threshold determined by 3 dB; the compressor will reduce the signal, and as a result, 1 dB will be obtained in the output instead of the 3 dB generated by the signal.

Again, if we adjust the threshold to 0 dB, instead of adding 3 dB to the signal, only 1 dB will be added. We will have a 2 dB reduction when the signal exceeds the threshold.

If the signal exceeds 6 dB and we have the same 3: 1 setting, the signal will be reduced by 4 dB, and as a result we will have 2 dB in the output instead of 6 dB. Let's see the following formula:

6 dB of input ÷ 3 (setting 3: 1) = 2 dB (2 dB will be added to the gain instead of 6 dB)

Let's see the following calculation by taking a 3: 1 adjustment

Adjustment 3:1

1. Signal that exceeds 3 dB (3 dB ÷ 3 = 1 dB)
2. Signal that exceeds 6 dB (6 dB ÷ 3 = 2 dB)
3. Signal that exceeds 9 dB (9 dB ÷ 3 = 3 dB)

The higher the number in the "Rate" setting, the more compression will be obtained. But we must be careful not to compress too much and we lose the naturalness of the signal.

<u>Atack - Release</u>

The ***attack*** tells us how fast the compressor will activate when it receives the signal, and the ***release*** determines how long the compression will remain before it runs out.

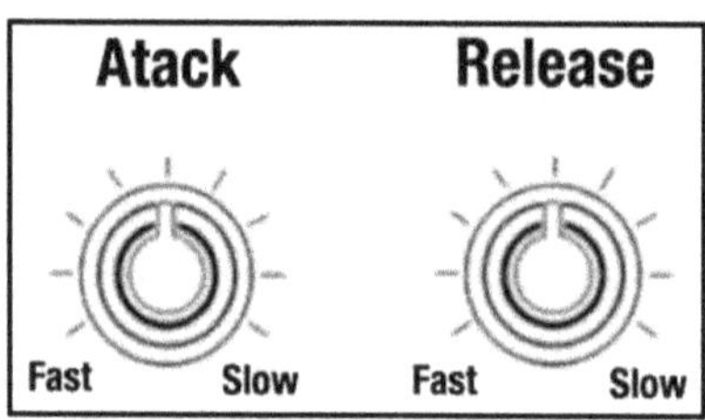


*Figure 20.5*

The graph in Figure 20.6 gives a better idea of how the compressor works.

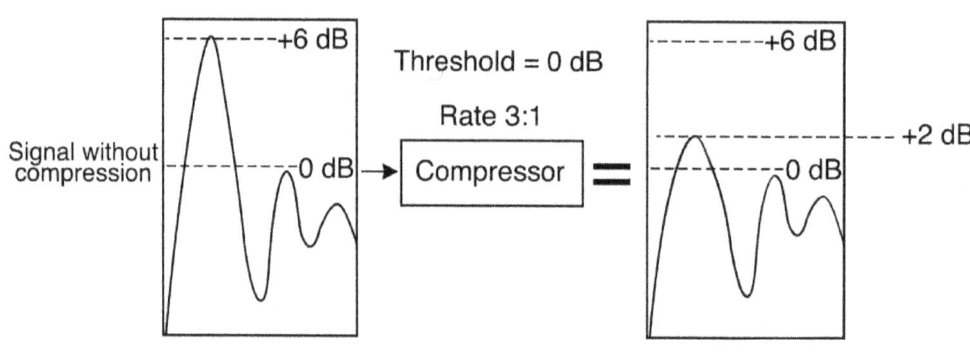


*Figure 20.6*

In Figure 20.7 we can see all the compressor settings, as we would see it in a digital way.

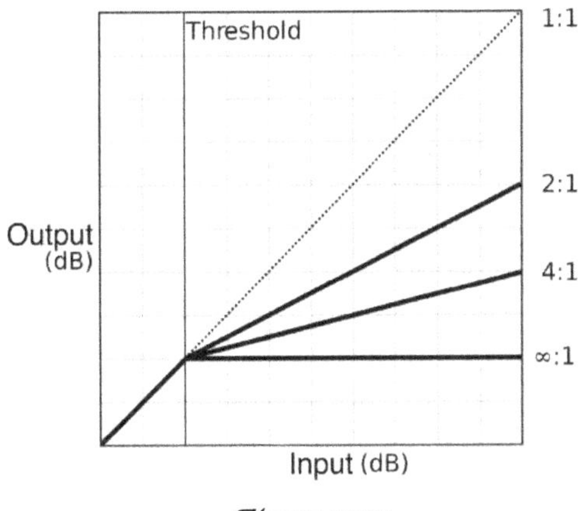


*Figure 20.7*

## Limiter

Adjusting the compression level in the 10: 1 position to infinity (represented by this symbol ∞), is considered to limit the signal. This is when we do not want the level of the signal to exceed a certain threshold.

If we compare the compressor and the limiter, the compressor will gently reduce the signal, but the limiter will do so aggressively. It's like putting a "stop" or a barrier to the signal.

## Compressor Connection

A. Using a cable for "insert" (Figure 19.13), the compressor can be connected in:
1. The "insert" of the channel.
2. The "insert" of the main output of the console.

***Remember that the "Tip" tip of the cable goes to the compressor inlet, and the "Ring" tip goes to the compressor outlet.***

B. Connecting the compressor in chain with other equipment and using ¼ unbalanced cables, can be connected:
1. From the output of the console, or from the output of a sub group, or from the output of an auxiliary.
    a. Procedure using the output of the console as an example.
        i. From the output of the console to the compressor inlet, and the compressor outlet to the other equipment inlet.

<u>Application</u>

1. A person who speaks softly, but has moments where he screams, and constantly needs to be adjusting the volume level in the console.

2. The drum "Kik" of the battery is played gently and suddenly very aggressive, having many variations in volume.

Limitation helps us not to let the signal go beyond a certain level. The limiter contains the same settings as the compressor, threshold, limiter selector (eg 10: 1), attack, release.

<u>Gate</u>

The gate acts as a signal switch. When the signal that enters the channel is strong, the gate opens; and when it is weak, it closes the passage of the signal.

When is the use of the gate necessary? Let's see the amplification of the drum. When a drum is amplified, several microphones are used to collect the different sounds coming from the drums and cymbals. Take the drummer's microphone to explain the example. The drummer generates a strong signal, which is usually for a short time. If the microphone is kept open, it will pick up the sounds of the other drums and cymbals. By inserting a gate, it will let the signal pass when it is strong and will close when it is weak (Figure 20.8).

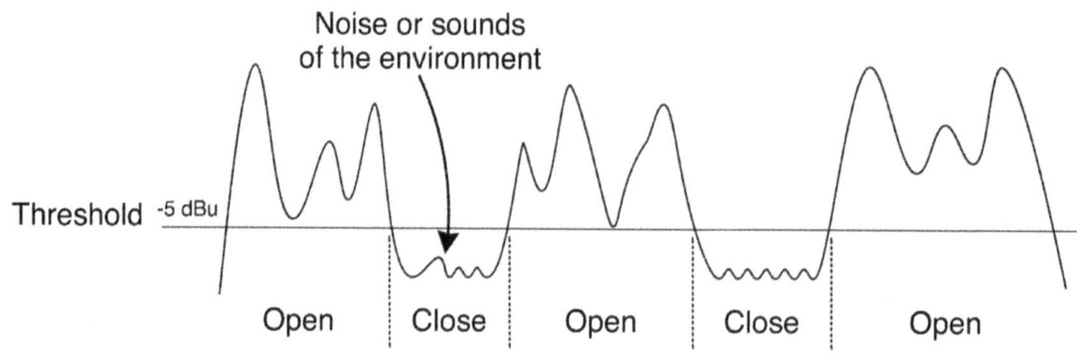


*Figure 20.8*

You must be very careful with the adjustments. Depending on where we place the threshold position, it may cause you not to open the gate in time and part of the signal will be lost. Also in the case of an instrument, there are sounds and effects that extend over a period that are important in the appreciation and, if the gate closes the channel very fast, the sound effect is lost.

Well used, it creates a clean mix and eliminates the possibilities of noise and feedback.

The adjustments made in the gate are:

1. Threshold adjustment
2. Time setting, fast or slow

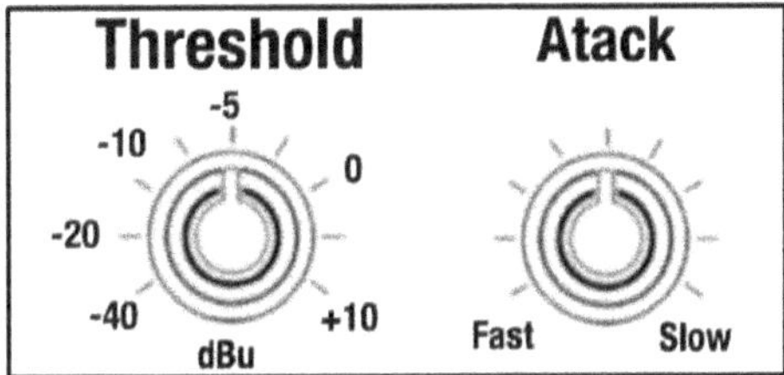


*Figure 20.9*

# Chapter 21: Effects

When we are in a space, either closed or open, we not only perceive the sounds as if they only come from the right or left side, but we also hear a third angle, which gives us the perception of depth.

This allows us to differentiate how we hear sounds in the different spaces in which we move every day. The sound we hear in a hallway is perceived differently than the one generated in a basketball court. A small room without acoustic treatment will allow us to hear the repetitions of our voice because of sound bouncing on the walls.

By listening to the sound in different spaces, we are naturally exposed to the effects known as reverberation, delays, echoes and all those reflections produced by the different surfaces. When applying effects to a signal in the console, we seek to simulate some of these spaces digitally, which in turn, add color and depth to the signal, and give the brain the perception of being in an interesting environment. That is why the use of the effects must be controlled, in an artistic way and looking for the liking of the listeners.

***A lot of effect on the signal can damage a mix.***

In Chapter 6, I talk about Local Acoustics where we play the theme of reverberation and echo.

Two of the effects widely used in a sound console, but which are not the only ones, are the delay and the reverb.


## Delay

What the "delay" does is create a copy of the original sound and an adjustment is made in the time between the original signal and the copy so that the copy is heard a little later. If the delay time setting is long, we will hear the repeat as an echo. The repetition of the original sound copy will continue for a certain time, depending on whether the delay setting is short or long, and it will dissipate as time passes.

The effects of "delay" has a button for adjusting the time. With it we can adjust the delay time to the speed of the song being played.

## Reverb

The *"reverb"* simulates the effect produced by the sound, when it bounces with the different surfaces in a room or closed place. We will find in the settings different types of reverb, simulating the size of the room or space. Some of the representative names of the different spaces are: chamber, small hall, large hall, plate.


## Dry and Wet

The terms *"dry"* and *"wet"* found in the effects equipment refer to the amount of effect that is determined to mix with the original signal. If we adjust more for the "dry" side, less effect will be mixed with the original signal and, on the other hand, if the adjustment is more for the "wet" side, there will be more mixed effects with the original signal.

# Chapter 22:  Adjusting the Audio System

Once you know how the graphic equalizer works, let's learn the process of adjusting our system.


## RTA – Real Time Spectrum Analyzer

To make an objective adjustment, it is necessary to use a ***real-time spectrum analyzer (RTA)***. The RTA is a measuring instrument that shows graphically, on a screen, the spectrum of a sound at each moment. On the screen, you can see the different frequencies by means of a bar graph and the sound pressure of each band (Figure 22.1).

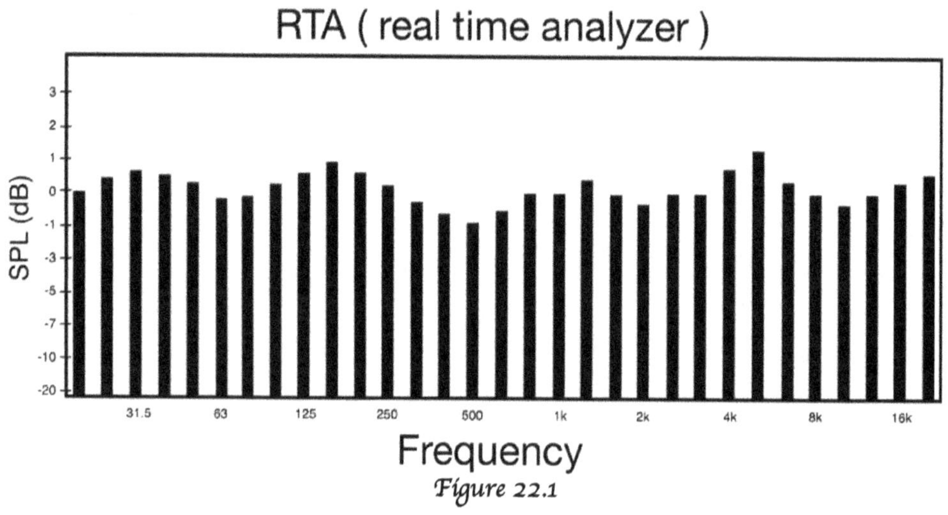


*Figure 22.1*

Before starting, all console controls should be brought to their central position. This means that the controls must be in the position where the gain is unitary, and the tone controls or equalizers in a flat position. The latter is important, since the equalization of the system should be considered as a reference adjustment, which means that a point of operation is established in which it is known that the response of the system is flat.

The following diagram in Figure 22.2 shows the way in which the connection should be carried out to make the adjustment.

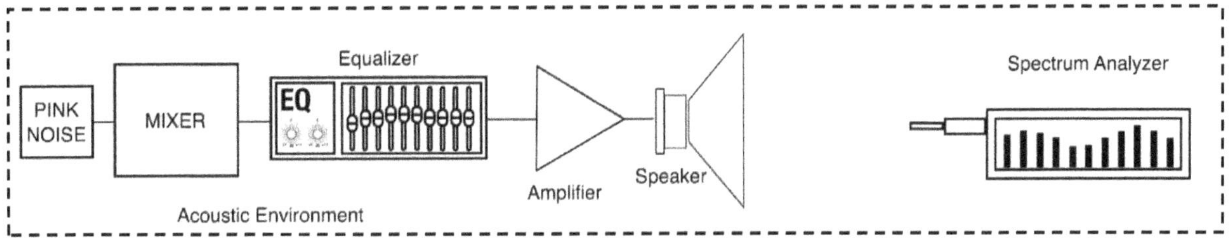


*Figure 22.2*

A pink noise signal is applied to an input of the console, which will pass through the equalizer, amplifier and finally out through the speaker.

## Pink Noise

Pink noise is a signal that contains the same amount of energy in each band, that is in each frequency. This allows the same indication or the same level to be obtained in all bands. Figure 22.3 is an example of the graph resulting from the measurement of some of our equipment, such as the console or an equalizer.

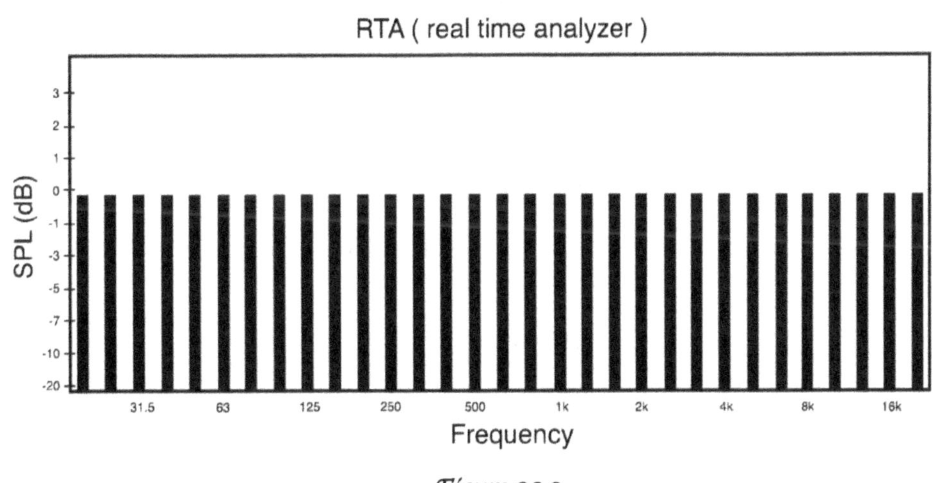


*Figure 22.3*

Then a microphone designed to perform audio measurements is placed in the position where the equalization is to be achieved, normally in the sound booth, and connected to the spectrum analyzer. A computer program is commonly used for measurement. The microphone will obtain the sound generated by the speakers and the sound resulting from the acoustic environment of the room.

The result of this measurement will give us an idea of how the frequencies of the sound system are heard at the point where the measuring microphone was placed. Finally, and depending on the result obtained with the measurement, the controls of the graphic equalizer are adjusted, to have an even indication in all the bands of the spectrum analyzer.

For example, suppose there is a dramatic increase between the 63Hz and 125Hz frequencies. With the equalizer, the keys corresponding to these frequencies will be adjusted to balance the sound in the room.

It is important to note that the image obtained on the analyzer screen is not static, and it will oscillate always. Visual averaging will be sought to obtain the flattest equalization of the system (Figure 22.4).

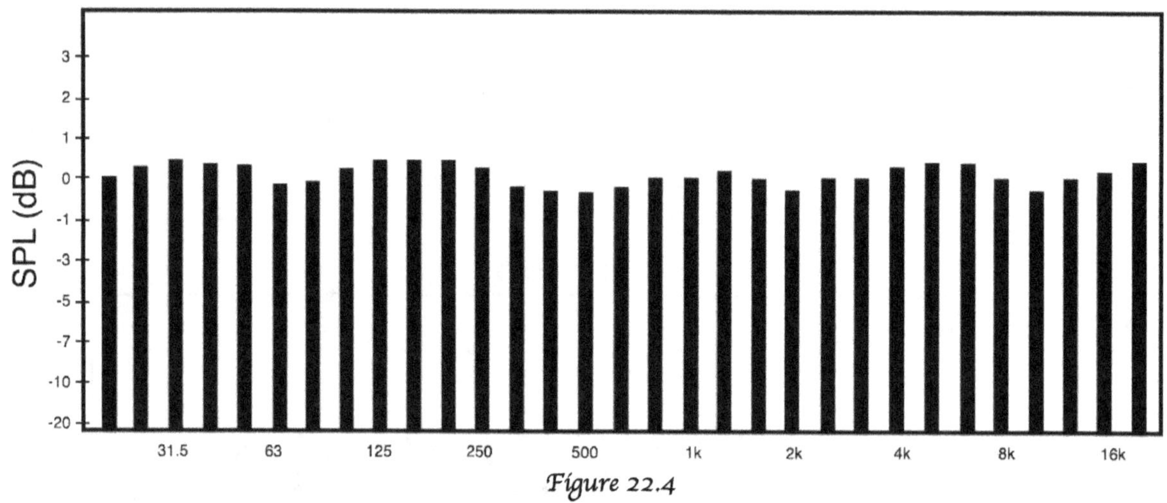

*Figure 22.4*

## Adjust the System without an RTA

Another process that is used to adjust the sound system is one of a personal nature, and will depend on the knowledge, tastes, appreciation, interpretation and audition of the sound engineer.

Normally, what is done is the following:

1. Once your sound system is installed, an audio recording made in a studio is used, with which you are familiar and where all the instruments are heard in a balanced way.

2. It is sought that the low, medium and high are heard evenly.

3. A musical genre where a frequency register predominates is not used.

# Conclusion

We have seen in this manual, how the topics have been exposed in a simple way, of fast application and with the aim of having a general knowledge about an audio system.

However, a window to live sound, aims to be a key that opens the door for each reader or student to deepen the topics discussed, and find resources in books, magazines, equipment manuals and sources available on the Internet, to expand your knowledge until you master and understand more deeply the information included here.

# Bibliography


Miyara, Federico. *"Acústica y Sistemas de Sonido"*. UNIR EDITORA. Editorial de la Universidad Nacional de Rosario. Urquiza 2050 – 2000 Rosario – República Argentina - 2000 (311 págs).

Hunter Stark, Scott. *"Live Sound Reinforcement: A Comprehensive Guide to P.A. and Music Reinforcement Systems and Technology"*. Mix Books. 236 Georgia Street, Ste. 100, Vallejo, CA 94590 – 1996-2000 (313 págs).

# About the Author

 José (Naldy) Resto, was born in Fajardo, Puerto Rico, and has had a musical career since he was 12 years old. He began his studies in the guitar, but then he dedicated himself to the bass, which gave him the opportunity to be part of different musical groups. He has participated in different studio recordings as a musician and producer, working with arrangers and composers such as Héctor "Perucho" Rivera and Richie Mejías. He has worked with theater musicals and has served as director, arranger and composer in different bands. He studied three (3) years of music studies at the Interamerican University of P.R., Metropolitan Campus.

In the year 2002, he opened his own music store with the name of Resto Music, where music classes, instrument repairs and sale and installation of sound equipment were offered.

Seeing the need to have a good sound in the bands where he played, he decides to venture into the world of professional audio, and for the last 15 years he has dedicated himself to the design, management and installation of sound systems for churches and venues. He has attended sound seminars in the United States, such as Sound System Optimization by Meyer Sound, Sound Reinforcement for Operators and Technicians of Synergetic Audio Concepts and obtained certification of Smaart Live software from Rational Acoustic.

He has mixed live sound to groups and singers like The Radicalled Movement, Nancy Amancio, Michael Rodriguez, Reynaldo Santiago "Chino", Song Institute of Puerto Rico, Xtremos Leaders, among others. He toured Puerto Rico with Daniel Calveti's ministry as a sound engineer and bassist.


"There are 3 factors that should follow a sound engineer wherever he is: humility, respect and the ability to learn and teach. In this way, day by day it will grow. "

*José (Naldy) Resto*